Tarot Journeys

Meditations by
Elizabeth Anderton Fox

Tarot Journeys

Meditations by
Elizabeth Anderton Fox

Stafford England

Tarot Journeys: Meditations by Elizabeth Anderton Fox
Elizabeth Anderton Fox
© 2021 First edition

All rights reserved, including the right to reproduce this book, or portions thereof, in any form, except for personal use, including group workshops. Authorship of this material must then be credited to Elizabeth Anderton Fox.

The rights of the individual to be identified as the author of this work have been asserted by them in accordance with the Copyright, Designs and Patents Act, 1988.

Editor: Danielle Lainton
Layout: Danielle Lainton
Cover Art and Design: Danielle Lainton

ISBN: 978-1-912241-22-4
Catalogue Number: MB0214

Set in Book Antiqua

A Megalithica Books Publication
An imprint of Immanion Press
http://www.immanion-press.com

Table of Contents

In Memory of my late husband John A.B. Fox, First Grand Master of the British Martinist Order.

Introduction

The Tarot is a pack of playing cards, used from the mid-fifteenth century in Europe to play games such as Italian Tarocchini. It consists of 78 cards divided into 22 Major Arcana and 40 Minor Arcana cards with 16 Court cards. Over time it has come to be used primarily as a means of divination but also for other mystical purposes. There are many different packs available to own that vary in their representation of the characters and style; it is therefore a matter of personal choice when deciding which pack is utilized for each individual. In this book I will be using the Major Arcana of the A.E. Waite pack but, as I said, it is a matter of personal preference which pack you choose to use, the symbolism is mainly the same in all packs. The techniques for following the meditations in this book are based around relaxation and quietness of the physical vehicle and calmness of the mind. The body should be seated in a comfortable upright position with the palms resting on the thighs. The breathing should be rhythmical and slightly slowed.

The purpose of these meditations is to gain access to the wisdom and knowledge concealed in the Tarot images. This will be revealed in a personal way through images and thoughts which arise during the course of the meditation. These are personal to each individual, there are no right or wrong results, the knowledge gained is appropriate to the needs of each person at that time. If desired a candle and incense may be used before meditation to create an atmosphere and a small ritual or prayer if desired. I have included a short opening and closing ritual, from *Journeys in the Light Within,* if you should desire to use it. I would highly recommend keeping a record of your meditations as results can often link up at a later date. Be aware that meditations are a little like dreams in that they tend to fade from memory very quickly however vivid and memorable they seem at the time. We will be setting out on a series of journeys and as our guides we will have the figures of the Tarot cards, we will meet them and learn from them. These figures will develop in our imagination and the images will provide a vehicle so that the deeper levels of our minds can be reached.

So to begin, allow an image of an old wooden door to form in your imagination and place a personal symbol of your choosing on the door the first time you use it, this will remain there throughout your journey. This is your access and exit image into and out of the inner worlds of the Tarot. Open the door and walk through. When you return seal the door with your symbol.

Following on from the end of the Tarot Journeys are some short pieces from my lecture notes on a few esoteric subjects. The literature on these topics is vast and often difficult to understand, hopefully the comments will be helpful in following the quest for the pearls of wisdom concealed in many of the ancient writings.

Solo Opening and Closing Ceremony Requirements

A secure and private small space

Small table for altar (round or square/oblong) and a comfortable but not easy chair.

Cloth to cover altar

Four small candles

Matches

Candle snuffer

Taper

Music player if desired

Ritual

Opening –

Prepare the Temple as in *diagram 1* at the end of this section.

Prepare yourself by washing hands and face.

Wear a plain ritual robe if desired.

Enter the temple and bow the head to the altar in recognition of its sacredness.

Taking lit taper, stand facing the altar

Be silent for a few minutes to still the mind then light

the first candle while saying,

Almighty Creative Powers, fill this place with Thy power and blessing.

Light second candle while saying,

Holy Powers of Knowledge and of Wisdom, teach me that I may grow.

Light third candle while saying,

Guides of the Inner Worlds bless my inner journeys that I may learn.

Light fourth candle while saying,

Sacred Powers of Earth bless my earthly life and my spiritual quest.

Bow to altar and be seated. Proceed with any work which is desired.

Closing -

When work is completed spend a few minutes in meditation of thanks.

Rise and stand in front of altar, taking candle snuffer.

Extinguish the first candle saying,

Almighty Creative Powers I thank you for your influence in this place.

Extinguish the second candle saying,

Holy Powers of Knowledge and of Wisdom, make clear my memory of your teachings.

Extinguish the third candle saying,

Guides of the Inner Worlds, accept my thanks and keep me in the knowledge of the inner ways.

Extinguish the fourth candle saying,

Sacred Powers of Earth bless my earthly life and my spiritual quest.

Bow to altar and depart.

Disrobe and spend a little time in silence. Take something to eat and drink.

Diagram 1

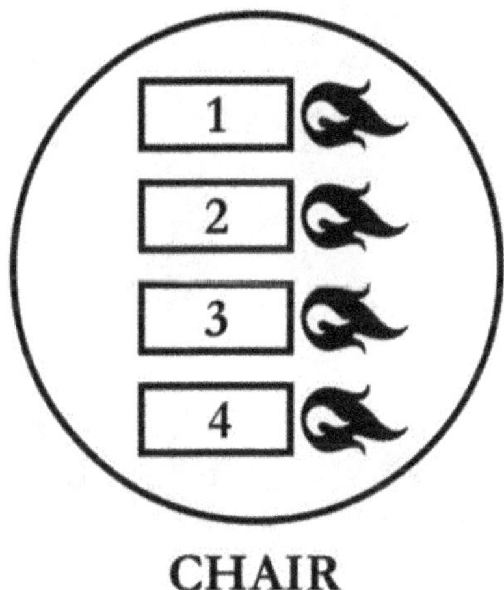

CHAIR

THE FOOL.

O
The Fool

Prepare for your first journey in the usual way, sit comfortably, relax and begin your rhythmical breathing.

Gradually your entry door begins to form in front for you, you see your symbol on the aged surface and push the door lightly, it swings open before you and you step through.

The scene you step into is of a bright sunny morning in a fresh beautiful green meadow glowing with the colours of a multitude of wildflowers.

This world is radiant, glowing and beautiful, and your walk across the meadow is full of joy. In the distance you can see vast mountains, and you realise that the meadow is actually on a high plateau. It is comfortably warm so it must be almost mid- morning. Looking around, at first, you seem to be the only person in this landscape, but no, there is a figure approaching. You cannot tell whether it is a young girl or a boy but they are tall and slim and walking with a lithe grace. At their heels bounces a little dog who constantly leaps up in joyful, playful affection. The figure draws nearer, smiles warmly and greets you cheerfully "Hello, I am The Fool, who are you?" A little taken aback you return the smile, and after a slight hesitation you explain that you are a visitor to these inner worlds. "Oh" he says, "Do you have a body in the material worlds?"

"Yes" you reply, "I am only here on a visit."

The Fool smiles again at you and says "I am on my

way to find my new body, it is pulling me very strongly now so I must be getting near to the border between this world and the material world. When I reach there and enter my new body I will begin another incarnation. Then this little dog will become my physical nature and guide me by the natural instincts of my body. I will need to learn how to rule him with wisdom. What is before you now is a created image which makes it possible for you to see me, it is not a reflection of a physical body as yours is." You are eager to learn more and ask if he has made this journey before. "Oh many, many times" says The Fool. He continues "I carry all my memories of my lives in this bag, I will share some with you if you like."

"Oh yes please" you say.

"Where shall we start?" says The Fool, then goes on. "I remember many lives but the beginning is too far away, so I will give you a general idea. Each body is different, sometimes I am male and sometimes female, sometimes I am blessed with a strong and healthy body, but occasionally I find myself having to deal with one which is impaired in some way which can be very hard, but which can teach me a lot. I have lived in many places on Earth and had bodies of many different colours, each one fitting me for the country in which I will dwell. I do not get a conscious choice which body I get, that is decided by the laws of Karma and what lessons I need to learn in a particular lifetime. Sometimes it is decided by the links I may have with others, who are also on the journey, and with whom I may have work to do or issues to resolve from previous lifetimes. Karma is the result of my actions in my previous lives, it is cause and effect. If I have done something silly, or even evil, Karma will give me the lessons I need to learn by my mistake. Equally a life well lived will result in the opportunities to live another good and useful life. The lessons of life are limitless.

For instance, we might find ourselves where we have great power and we have to learn how to handle this wisely. Power and great comfort can be very seductive and can lead us into idleness and depravity. But in all these experiences we have the inner guide of our memory which speaks to us with the still small voice within, be sure to listen to its advice.

Each lifetime we start out with a new body, if we are fortunate it is healthy and whole. Our body is a precious gift from the Universe and it is our responsibility to care for it, to treat it with respect and never abuse it in act or deed. Likewise, we should treat the bodies of others with the same respect we give our own.

They name me The Fool and perhaps I am, for indeed I have often been foolish, but sometimes the wise wear the outward guise of the fool to protect them from the ill will of the truly foolish and ignorant. If you have a good body treasure and value it. If your life is successful guard it with care. What else would you like me to tell you?"

"I would like to know more about memory" you say.

The Fool smiles and says "Memory is the record of the entire contents of every life you have lived, it is also the collective record of everyone else and of the Universe in which we live. As you can imagine this is immense so it is not surprising that we do not have access to it all, it would be too overwhelming. However, we can have access to part of our personal memory. When we reincarnate we start anew and our memories are sealed from us.

This amnesia is necessary for full memory of our lives would be too heavy a burden to bear and we would be overcome with sorrow for old loss and regrets for past mistakes. Our memories surface in what we call instinctive knowing, sometimes they manifest as talents for things we have learnt in previous lives as is the case with great musicians or others of great talent. Those things which come easily to us are from our remembering, it is those we are meeting for the first time that we find difficult. I must be on my way now for I feel the urgency and pull of my new body. It is coming very close to birth now. Soon I will once more make the leap off this plateau and fall into manifestation. Be well my friend and enjoy your visit to these realms. Farwell."

And with a last wave of the hand The Fool springs forward across the meadow and disappears into the sunlight and the distance.

You feel the pull of your own body calling to you to return, you turn and walk back the way you came and presently your door appears in the sunlight before you. You touch it and it opens, you walk through and find yourself back in your own time and place.

I
THE MAGICIAN.

I
The Magician

Prepare for the journey in your usual way.

Let the old wooden door form in front of you, open it and walk through.

You find yourself on a cobbled path that is sloping away gently in front of you. You amble down the street admiring the picturesqe buildings on either side. On your right you notice an archway, it looks interesting so you walk through and find yourself in the quadrangle of a scholastic building. Ancient walls are on every side of you enclosing a central grassy area. There is a peaceful atmosphere about this place and you wander around for a time enjoying being here.

After a short while you observe an open door with an advertisment pinned to it. You go closer to see what it says and read that there is to be a talk by The Magician. This awakens your interest especially as it says 'All Welcome No Charge'..You enter through the doorway and walk down a short corridor, at the end of which is another door which again you enter. You find yourself in a small lecture theatre with a half circle of tiered seats and a low stage, raised enough for the speaker to be seen but low enough for them to blend with the audience. On the stage is a small table covered with a white cloth. There is already a small audience so your find yourself a seat a few rows from the front.

After a short wait a figure enters and stands behind the small table near the front of the stage. He is tall and slim and of middle years. He wears a plain white ritual gown under a flowing red robe. About his waist is the cord of his rank. He looks around the assembled audience as if he would weigh up each one of us, then reaches out both hands and gives a slight bow of his head.

"Greetings Companions" he says. "I am The Magician and I would like to talk to you today about what it means to be a Magician; it means that one is a master of magic. But then we have to define what magic is, an important point since there are so many misconceptions regarding this word. The most common is that the Magician can cause effects to happen by his will that are contrary to natural law. This is not true. Events only appear to be magical when the laws invoked to bring about effects are unknown to the observer. The Magician is one who knows the laws behind effects and uses this knowledge to bring about desired results. There are many events in our daily lives which appear magical because we have not yet discovered the laws which rule them. But be assured the Universe and everything within it functions according to Law. This applies to both the physical and mental functions of a manifested being be they human or animal.

The Magician is the achytype of the human male and symbolises the Laws which rule him. Within nature all things function according to Law, these Laws are consistent and dependable. These symbols on my table represent the powers and the Laws which they rule". He walks to the small table and points to the symbols which you had not previously noticed. Picking up the first he continues.

"The Wand is the symbol of, and the key to, the powers of Fire. It symbolises will and intent, energy, action, competition and power: metaphysically, it represents, enlightenment, awareness, intuition, inspiration and higher consciousness. It is the conductor of higher powers to the lower. Raised in my right hand it conducts these powers through my down pointing left hand into the level of Earth. By understanding these powers of Fire I can focus them to a particular end result."

Going again to the table he replaces the Wand and picks up the Sword and continues.

"The Sword is the symbol of, and the key to, the powers of Air. It symbolises power, protection, authority, strength, and courage; metaphysically, it represents discrimination and the penetrating power of the intellect. It is also the conductor of initiatic authority from Initiator to candidate. It is the defender on both the physical and the spiritual levels. By understanding these powers of Air I can focus them to a particular end result."

Going again to the table he replaces the sword and picks up the chalice.

"The Chalice is the symbol of, and the key to, the powers of Water. It symbolises intuition, elevation, sensuality, and completeness. Metaphysically it represents purification and transformation, living and healing, energy and manifestation. It is generally shaped as a goblet on a stem and a rounded base. There are many other meanings especially in esoteric and religious practices. It is regarded as the Holy Grail. Its contents are regarded as sacred and its function is to bestow a blessing when drunk from, especially in ceremony. It also symbolises the Sacred Quest or Journey."

Going again to the table he replaces the chalice and picks up the platter. "The platter is the symbol of Earth, with the pentacle drawn on its surface being the symbol of humanity. It symbolises matter, humanity, fertility, infinite creativity, and longevity. Metaphysically it represents intellect and reason.

These four symbols represent the sphere of magical practice on the different levels of being.

The Wand - The will of the Practitioner

The Sword - The Intellect which organises the actions.

The Cup - which empowers the actions through the emotions.

The Platter - the physicality which operates the actions of the magic.

Magic is mental. It functions through the imagination.

It is important to remember that all experiences happen within the mind, whether they appear to arise in the outer or inner spheres of consciousness. These are the keys to magic. It is the work of the apprentice magician to learn what the laws behind their functioning are and to apply them with discretion and wisdom.

Thank you for your attendance. I wish you good day."

The Magician bows his head briefly, turns and leaves the stage. You and the rest of the audience rise and slowly leave the lecture theatre and make your way outside. For a time you wander around the building thinking of what you have just heard, Then making your way back into the street you walk a little way then see the old door with your symbol upon it, you push it open and walk through back into your own time and place.

II
B
J
TORA
THE HIGH PRIESTESS

II
The High Priestess

Prepare for the journey in the usual manner.

Let the old wooden door form in front of you, open it and walk through.

You walk through the door and find yourself surrounded by a swirling violet mist which disorientates you a little. The mist clears and you find yourself seated in a softly lit room. It is a large rectangular room, its walls decorated in pale violet with a few beautiful pictures of moonlit scenes and of the sea. At one end of the room is a low dais, on it is a woman, seated on a throne like chair. She is beautiful and of mature years, her face radiating garnered wisdom. On either side of her is a pillar and below her feet a large crescent moon. On her breast is an equal armed cross and she is crowned with the Moon Crown. Her hands rest in her lap holding two scolls which are the records of her experience. She turns and looks towards you "Welcome student of the Mysteries" she says. "Today it is the time for one of our young apprentice Priestesses to be examined so that she may establish her right to proceed in her training. You are welcome to stay and be witness to her examination with her blessing and mine" You rise and express your thanks for the privilage and are seated again. After a while of silence you catch a movement at the far end of the hall and turning you see a young woman dressed all in white approching the throne. She advances and standing in front of the Lady places her right hand over her heart and bows in reverence.

The Lady says. "Welcome Priestess. Why do you come here this day?"

"To be examined to see if I am ready to pass to the next stage of my training" says the young Priestess.

There then follows a dialogue between them.

The Lady begins;

"What is my Office?"

"You are the High Priestess, the Mistress of Magic. You are the archytype of the human female and symbolise the Laws which rule her."

"What is magic?"

"It is the knowledge and use of natural Law in order to achive a desired manifest result."

"Where does my magic function?"

"It functions in the realm of the mind and emotions."

"What are the names of the two pillars which stand on my right hand and upon my left?"

"They are named Wisdom and Strength, for it is those qualities which you symbolise. A Priestess must learn from the lessons of life and from the knowledge of her predecessors that she in her turn may become the Teacher to others. She must also learn to be strong so that she may be capable of standing alone in her knowledge and capable of withstanding the abuse of the ignorant. The pillars also represent the opposites of life between which she must function. They represent the balance of function between yourself and The Magician."

"What does the equal armed cross upon my breast symbolise?"

"The cross in its many forms has always

symbolised the Divine. It is a symbol of what is held sacred in a thousand different forms, which are in essence and truth all one. Its four arms also symbolise the Four Elements which are the traditional foundation of magic".

"Why is there a crescent Moon beneath my feet?"

"Because you rule the Powers of Water and the Moon rules the ebb and flow of the tides of the sea and life on Earth."

"What is symbolised by the Moon Crown upon my head?"

"It is the sign of your Office, it represents feminine energy. It signifies control of the cycles of the seas, of fertility and growth and of the life force within humans and animals."

"What do the symbols on the veil behind me symbolise?"

"They symbolise the power you hold. The pomegranates are symbols of plenty, of life and of death. The palm symbolises victory, peace, and eternal life."

"What do the scrolls held on my lap contain?"

"They contain the records of all that you govern. They tell of the powers of intuition, the still small voice by which you communicate with the sons and daughters of humanity. They tell of the powers that rule births and of deaths, the cycles of all lives. They tell too of the laws which govern the cycles of lives, the laws of reincarnation and the links which join our many lives.

You are the spiritual Mother of Earth and all its inhabitants. You are the High Priestess of The Mystery and the holder of higher powers. Your scrolls inform of the secrets of the subconscious mind, of wisdom and great knowledge. You hold the key to illumination and the completion of The Journey."

"You have spoken well. Go hence my Daughter in Light and know that you may now enter the next phase of your learning with my blessing."

The Priestess once more salutes the High Priestess and bows. She turns and leaves the room the way she came.

Then the High Priestess once more addresses you. "So are each of us tested at each stage of our learning. Do not be distressed by the trials which you encounter on your journey but learn the lesson of each one well. For life is as the waves of the sea, the troughs may be deep yet they are they always followed by the crest of the wave. It is time now for you to return to your own level. Go with my blessing and be at peace."

You rise, salute and bow to the High Priestess then turn and leave the room. You are once again in the violet mist, your door forms before you, you walk through and are once more back in your own time and place.

III
THE EMPRESS.

III
The Empress

Prepare in your usual way for the journey.

Let the old door form in front to you and go through.

You find yourself in a beautiful forest glade, before you there are tall trees on either side of a pathway half covered in grass and leaves. The sun shines through the leafy canopy and makes dappled patterns on the path. The trees are still in leaf but there are touches of autumn colours here and there. The trees are not too close together, this has allowed enough light to reach the ground so that a scattering of wildflowers has been able to blossom and add a dash of vibrant colour to the scene. You begin to walk following the path. A little while on you notice another path joining the one you are following; it joins yours on your left.

You spot a young woman just about to join your path, she is accompanied by two young children, they are so alike and similar in size you guess they must be twins but not identical for one is a girl and the other a boy. The little family smile and greet you, the children dancing about in excitement. The young woman is slightly matronly in appearance but has a warm and welcoming air about her. You walk along with her, chatting as you go. She tells you that the children are indeed hers and they are twins and almost five years in age. She explains that they are heading to a special place in the forest because The Empress is making a visit and all who wish to are welcome to see her. You feel an upsurge of excitement at the prospect of seeing

The Empress. You carry on together and the young woman tells you that The Empress helped her when she and her husband were having problems conceiving.

It is not long before you hear the sounds of a crowd gathering, people, animals, and birds. When you emerge from the trees, they all are in a large clearing in the forest and across from you is The Empress seated on a throne like chair upon a small mound. She is dressed in a long flowing robe embroidered with red roses, the symbol of love and desire. It is also the sub-rosa symbol of confidentiality and secrecy. The sound of fast flowing water comes from somewhere behind her. In her right hand she carries a sceptre with the orb of the Earth surmounting it. At her right foot is a heart shared shield bearing the sign of Venus which symbolise her dominion over the heavens and the feminine powers.

She is surrounded by the growth of the forest, trees, grasses, flowers, and fruit bearing plants. All around her are animals, small and large, birds and bees, insects and butterflies, and at her feet is a field of golden corn ripe for harvesting. The crowd is full of people of all ages and races, at least one representative of each.

You find a log on which to sit and the four of you settle down to enjoy the assembly.

The Empress surveys us all with a sweet smile. She begins to speak but it is as if she speaks within your mind so each word seems meant especially for each of us. "Welcome my children" she says "It is my privilege to be with you for this gathering. My message today is this, hear and remember. My dominion is over all living things human, animal, bird, fish, plants, trees insects, microbes, and microscopic life forms. With equal justice and without favour I rule them all. I hold the key to entrance into this world for I am Isis, Demeter and Mary. I am the Great Mother who opens the gate to all who pass through into life. I watch over the growing seed and the hatching egg, I guard the child in the womb of all species.

Know that all within the Divine Universe operates according to Divine Law. While a species operates efficiently it can remain stable for millions of years. When a different need arises in their environment the Creative Source and the evolutionary powers are unlocked to make the necessary changes. Throughout the manifest Cosmos, which is constantly evolving, the law is the same, efficient forms are stable; unstable or unsatisfactory ones invoke the law of 'Need creates Change.'

The Earth is a self- sustaining eco system where of necessity one species preys upon another. If the demands of one predator become too heavy upon one species, then in my justice I guide the victims to a safer living space until time has restored their numbers. Humanity has established an unprecedented control over the environment which comes with a responsibility to care for it and see it is not harmed. Learn my laws and give the Earth and its creatures the same care as I would do myself. Be my ambassadors and work in my name. In the vastness of the Universe the Earth is a precious jewel, see that it remains so. Go with my blessing."

As The Empress ceases speaking the watchers

begin to move towards her, she has words for each one, a touch of the hand here and a smile there. All are enfolded in her warmth and love. You wait for the crowd to thin then go forward, she greets you with a smile and holds out her hand and blesses you. A great sense of warmth and peace floods through you, you bow and turn to leave.

You find your way back to the path by which you came and begin to retrace your steps through the forest. You linger here and there to think over what The Empress said and to feel again in memory the power of her blessing. As you continue your walk you see ahead of you the old wooden door, you approach it and it swings open, you walk through and find yourself back in your own time and place.

IV
THE EMPEROR.

IV
The Emperor

Prepare in your usual way for the journey.

As you relax the outer world begins to fade, then in front of you your old wooden door begins to form. You push the door open and walk through.

You find yourself in a beautiful mountain scene. All about you are mountain tops soaring into the sky and far below are the verdant valley floors. A brilliant sun shines over the whole scene.

Then, improbable as it might seem - but after all this is the inner world where anything is possible - you see on the very summit of the highest mountain there is a seated figure. He is a bearded man of mature years with a strong physique; he wears a robe like garment of deep red over martial armour which can just be seen on his legs and arms. On his head he wears a golden crown decorated with jewels. In his right hand he holds a sceptre which is crowned with the ancient symbol of the crux ansata, the symbol of eternal life. In his left hand he holds the orb, symbol of his dominion over Earth.

The throne like chair on which he is seated, is decorated above his head and under his hands with the heads of rams. The rams are also an associated symbol of Mars the ancient god of war and conflict. These are the symbols of masculinity, lordship, authority in his role as a ruler. They are the symbols of masculine drive, virility, and power in his role as a lover and father. They are the symbols of authority, bravery, and energy in his role as a warrior and commander. His whole bearing is one of strength, rulership and dominance. You recognise him as The Emperor who rules over the material world. He is the masculine equivalent of The Empress and shares her power over the natural world, he is the drive which causes the males of all species to seek a mate and generate the next generations. He is the force in the bees and insects which cause them to pollinate the plants so that seeds may be fertile.

Then a movement catches your eye, you see a column of men and women climbing towards The Emperor, winding their way along a path which snakes up the side of the mountain. Leading the procession is a company of knights dressed in armour, behind them, as far as you can see, is a long column of people of every country and race, for The Emperor rules over them all. Eventually the knights arrive in front of the seated Emperor, each pair stops in front of him they halt, turn to face him, and then salute. As the Knights move on and as the people arrive in front of The Emperor they too turn and salute or bow, then take their place in the long ranks facing him. The procession seems to take a long time to complete their assembly but at last all are in place and await The Emperor's address. He rises and salutes them in return, then addresses them all.

"My children one and all. It is with great pleasure that I welcome you here this day. It is not often that we assemble thus but I have an important message for you this day. As you know I am responsible for the masculine aspects of the natural forms of Earth, this includes every living species, human, animal, fish, bird, insect, and plant. I rule over the natural forces that control the functions of the sea, land, and skies of Earth. I hold the balance of these forces whether it be weather, fire, or volcanic eruptions. And it is of this responsibility for balance that I wish to speak to you this day.

While I hold this power I exercise it through the agency of natural Law and the work of nature and its species. I am sure you are not unaware that there are aspects of Earth which are out of balance at this time. This is causing many problems in the weather and the natural world. It is a sad fact that humanity is responsible for many of these problems. Over the past century humanity has made great progress in learning how to prevent early death of both infants and adults. You have learnt how to prevent and cure diseases and many ways to give people a much longer life span. As a result populations have grown at a faster rate than has been seen for many centuries, if at all. This increase has meant a vast increase in the life needs of humanity.

A need for more space to live and for meeting the needs for food, which are putting great pressure on the worlds of animals and agricultural foods. And sorry to say this has too often not met with increased planning and wise husbandry. Too often resources are put under pressure by taking more than is needed. The resources of the Earth are not limitless.

It is necessary to consider how Earth can continue to sustain increasing populations, you have the means to control this in your grasp.

You have become inventive in a remarkable way and the technology you now command is presenting the world with immense opportunities. But you do not consider how you are polluting the planet with the refuse of your inventions. Nor is this limited to the Earth but extends to the heavens where you leave discarded items to pollute space.

My Children it is time and more than time to consider these things. I come to give you warning that if you do not restore balance the powers of nature will do so for you."

The Emperor rises and facing the vast throng raises his hands in blessing. "Go forth my children and may your endeavours to restore balance prosper."

Then as we watch the form of The Emperor gradually fades before our eyes and his apparent form becomes once more invisible energy.

The vast crowd begins to scatter and descend the mountain. You watch their progress and think on the words you have heard.

Then you feel the pull of your own place and your presence at this level begins to fade and your old doorway starts to form before your eyes. It swings open and you go forward and walk though back into your own time and place.

V
THE HIEROPHANT

V
The Hierophant

Prepare in your usual way for the journey.

As you relax the outer world begins to fade then in front of you your old wooden door begins to form. You push the door open and walk through.

You find yourself in a beautiful hall, it is not large but its proportions make it appear so. On the walls at either side of you, and behind you on either side of the doorway, are beautiful tapestries. They are large and cover most of the depth of the walls. They depict the wise Masters who were the founding inspiration for some of the world's great religions. There are depictions of Jesus, Buddha, Mohammed, Zoroaster, Lao Tzu, Moses, and many others, maybe in imagined representations but potent in their effects. At the far end of the hall on a raised dais sits The Hierophant between two large pillars. These pillars represent Law and Liberty and sometimes Obedience and Disobedience. His face is rather feminine in appearance which would indicate that the role could be filled by either a man or a woman. He wears a loose deep red garment over a white under robe. On his head he wears the triple-crown which is the symbol of his authority over the heads of organised religions. In his left hand he holds a staff surmounted by a triple cross, on which the three bars represent the Father, Son and the Holy Spirit or Spirit, Soul and Body. The Cross is about eternal Life because it is the Tree of Life of the Kabbala. His right hand is raised in the ecclesiastical sign of blessing and benediction. This sign of the raised first two fingers and the lowered last two fingers is also known as the sign of esotericism and of exoteric doctrine. At his feet are the crossed keys which represent his authority over spiritual life and are said to represent the keys of heaven. Around his neck he wears the stole of office of his function which is embroidered with crosses symbolising his spiritual role.

Before him kneel two priests or acolytes. The robe of one bears the roses of love and sub rosa significance and the other bears the lilies of devotion and purity.

You realise you have been studying him for some time and you are not altogether surprised when his gaze turns towards you as he has obviously noticed your presence. He leans forward and speaks to the two acolytes before him. They rise and lean towards him to listen then turn and begin to walk down the hall towards you. You rise to meet them wondering if you are to be asked to leave the hall, instead they arrive before you and tell you that His Holiness gives you greetings and has sent them to answer any of your questions.

You thank them and think what you would like to say, "What is his main function?" you ask.

"He is the Spiritual Father of humanity, he is their teacher and their councillor, responsible for their teaching and learning of religion. He is head of all religions in the world."

"Please tell us more of religion you say." And they continue-

"It is in the nature of every human being, wherever he or she may be born, to feel an urge towards the Divine and the mysteries of the unseen worlds. Even in the most primitive communities there is always one who sees deeper into the unseen than others. This one will become the shaman or medicine man of the community. In time the forces they see around them become personalised into Beings with powers over the forces of nature who can be petitioned for protection or knowledge. Religion is the expression of these basic instincts.

In time a Wise One will be born who will take the community on to the next stage of spiritual growth. These Masters have appeared at different stages in our history. Think of the stories of Zoroaster, Buddha, Jesus, or Mohammed, how they lived an Earth life and passed on their teachings to the people of their time. So powerful are their words that many are moved to record and follow their teachings. Gradually more and more followers take up their words which then become formalised into a religion. As time passes the more powerful personalities rise to influence in the community and begin to formalise the religion, thus arises dogma. This process becomes stronger until eventually spiritual power becomes political worldly power and the founder's words begin to be forgotten.

To follow a sincere religion is a necessary stage on the path of spiritual growth."

You say your thanks and ask your next question.

"What are the main functions of religions?"

They continue "Well first of all they provide an outlet for the spiritual aspirations of humanity, a way to express devotion to the Divine and to partake in mutual prayer and ceremony. The emotions generated by religious practice have produced some of the greatest works of art and literature. Then also as expressions of their faith different cultures have built magnificent churches, cathedrals, and temples in honour of their God. Religions have always played an important part in forming the ethics of societies. Teaching the young the difference between right and wrong and the adults what is acceptable and unacceptable behaviour.

Finally, they awake a desire to experience the deeper levels of consciousness and set the soul on the great quest of the spirit."

They place their hands over their hearts and bow to you and you know that our time with them is ended. They turn and leave the hall.

With one last long look around the hall and at The Hierophant you turn and walk towards the door, as you get near to it you realise it is not the door to the hall but to your own entry door. You gently push it open and walk through back into your own time and place.

VI
THE LOVERS.

VI
The Lovers

Prepare in your usual way for the journey.

As you relax the outer world begins to fade then in front of you your old wooden door begins to form. You push the door open and walk through.

You find yourself in a very beautiful garden, it is lovelier than anything you have ever seen. Before you are flower beds filled with roses of all colours and other beds overflowing with blooms of every description. On either side the display rises, first with bushes then gradually into trees of increasing height. As you walk on you pass a large pond in which numerous golden fishes swim. It feels as though you are then coming to the end of the garden but no, you are now in an orchard where all varieties of fruit are growing. You eventually reach a grassy area and see before you a man and a woman standing in front of trees a few feet apart from each other. Both are unclothed but seem quite unaware of the fact. The woman stands before the Tree of Knowledge and twined about its trunk is a serpent which is the symbol of wisdom and truth. The man stands before the Tree of Life which bears twelve fruits significant of many powers in nature and in alchemy. Behind them and at some distance rises a volcanic shaped mountain, symbolic of the powerful forces which animate them.

As you watch them you realise that they are Adam and Eve. They represent the first man and woman who by their coming together generated children and all the races of the Earth. They are the primal parents of humanity standing in the Garden of Eden.

The same force which brings them together also drives every creature on the planet to seek a mate and to raise the next generation

Above the scene a great golden sun shines down, its rays spreading far and wide and showering everywhere with its life-giving warmth and energy. It reminds us that nothing can flourish without the Sun. Below the Sun and above the man and woman a mighty angelic figure, crowned with flames, rises from a bank of clouds. With outspread wings and hands raised in blessing it seems to transmit the life of the Sun to them and fill them with its fertility.

This is the Archangel Gabriel, the messenger of God, who traditionally announces the imminent birth of the Teachers of the ages.

Then the scene changes, the garden fades from view and all that remains are the man and woman standing against the golden sunlight. They are now clothed splendidly in regal robes and crowned with golden circlets. They are the alchemical King and Queen whose union brings about the fusion of opposites, the two polarities, male and female, that live within each of us. It is the destiny of these polarities to seek union and not to remain separate. This is an internal process that unites the sacred feminine in union with the sacred masculine. When we balance these polarities into union within, we create balance and harmony in our inner and outer world. The process of this integration of the two polarities is called in Alchemy, The Great Work, the Alchemical Marriage of the King and the Queen.

There are seven principles which guide the Great Work. As stated in the Kybalion, a Hermetic text, these are:

1. **Mentalism** - The All is mind; the Universe is mental.

2. **Correspondence** - As above, so below, as below, so above.

3. **Vibration** - Nothing rests; everything moves; everything vibrates.

4. **Polarity** - Everything is dual; everything has poles; everything has its pair of opposites.

5. **Rhythm** - The pendulum-swing manifests in everything; the measure of the swing to the right is the measure of the swing to the left; rhythm compensates.

6. **Cause & Effect** - Every Cause has its Effect; every Effect has its Cause.

7. **Gender** - Gender is in everything; everything has its Masculine and Feminine Principles; Gender manifests on all planes

These principles tell us how the world and ourselves as human beings work, each one is a key which unlocks knowledge. Study them and you will understand.

Once again the scene changes, the King and Queen

move towards each other and blend into a single figure which becomes absorbed into the golden light of the Sun.

Then out of the sunlight walk two figures, a man and a women clothed in modern day dress. They walk towards you holding hands as they come and talking quietly together. They notice your presence and smile at you. They stop to chat and tell you they have been celebrating the anniversary of their marriage. They say that they are so fortunate to have found each other and tell you what a blessing they have in their life, that they share a love which enriches their lives every day. They walk a little way with you and the garden begins to form around you again. Then they go their way together and you turn to see your old door forming in front of you, you go through and find yourself once more back in your familiar time and place.

VII
THE CHARIOT.

VII
The Chariot

Prepare for the journey in your usual way.

As you relax the outer world begins to fade then in front of you your old wooden door begins to form. You push the door open and walk through.

You find yourself standing at the edge of a wide-open space, it looks like a parade ground. On the far side you can see a wide fast flowing river and on the far bank the towers of a city.

Then you hear the sounds of an advancing army. They appear on your left, first there are foot soldiers in their best ceremonial uniform, then the military band, not playing now except for the regular beat of the drums. The soldiers arrange themselves around the edges of the ground, then a troop of men mounted on very smart horses come trotting in and take their places in front of the foot soldiers. The band sounds a trumpet call and here enters the Commander in his chariot. He rides around the ground and comes to a halt in the middle and facing in your direction. The chariot is a splendid affair with a canopy decorated with stars signifying his authority. Drawn by two sphinx like creatures wearing the nemes headdress, the sign of the Commander's authority and power. One of the creatures is black and the other white which indicates they are the powerful opposition forces combined.

The Commander stands in his chariot radiating confidence, determination, and strength. He is dressed in ceremonial armour, at his shoulders are the signs of the crescent Moon, signifying his rule over the forces of time and the favour of ancient goddesses. In his right hand he holds a wand like staff which is the emblem of his authority, and on his head he wears the laurel and stars crown of victory. On the front of the chariot is a winged sun, the symbol of royalty and power. Below it is a shield bearing a spindle like symbol which may signify his ability to control the threads of power. The Commander may well be of royal blood but his authority is not inherited it is won by his own superiority and ability. The spheres of his conquests are external in the manifest world and not spiritual ones within himself. He is the epitome of victory and triumph. As you watch, the horses and riders and the foot soldiers form a procession. The band begins to play a marching tune and they circle the Commander three times before marching out of the arena. Finally the Commander who has stood at attention in his chariot saluting the procession, moves off and follows them out. It is suddenly very silent.

Gradually the scene begins to fade in front of you, all you can see is a heavy mist. Then a new scene begins to form, you see a small room comfortably furnished with large windows through which the sunlight floods in. You notice someone seated in one of the comfortable chairs, he looks somewhat familiar, he turns his head and you recognise the acolyte of The Hierophant who spoke to you. He sees you and beckons you to come forward into the room, you do so and step before him with a slight bow of respect. He acknowledges your greeting and indicates that you should be seated near him, you gratefully take the chair he indicates. For a little while he speaks of the recent ceremony and its pomp and display then he becomes serious. "His Holiness wishes me to speak to you of the role of the Commander and his chariot." he says and continues, "You see the Commander demonstrates the power of military and political power. But to sustain his hold on this power he must also have control over his own personality. He must be strong in his ethics and his understanding of those under his leadership. He must endeavour to use his power for the best good of those whose lives he controls. Power can be very seductive and sway one into believing one's own desires are of primary importance. As it has been said 'power corrupts and absolute power corrupts absolutely.' So such a one must constantly be on guard against their baser instinct. It is one of the more difficult tests of spiritual growth, whether one can handle the challenges and trials of power in the material world." He pauses and we think over what he has said for we had not considered the tests behind the glamour of the Commander.

He continues "Then there is the symbolic meaning of the Chariot. It is not just a vehicle in which the Commander rides. It is the body in which you ride the adventures of your life's incarnation. If you care for it and treat it respectfully it will serve you efficiently and well. Do not abuse it by overindulgence in the pleasures of life. The opposites which are represented by the creatures drawing the chariot will serve you well, but be warned you need to keep them balanced for if one gains the upper hand they can pull you far off your path. You can ride in your chariot to a successful life and give yourself time too to devote to your inner spiritual life also. Be honourable in all your dealings and you will be as successful as the Commander is in his sphere. Now my time with you draws to a close, drive well and true. Farewell and blessings be with you."

As he falls silent he and the room begin to fade before you and you feel the pull of your own place. You rise and find your door forming behind you, you turn and walking towards it push the door open and walk through, back into your own time and place.

VIII
STRENGTH.

VIII
Strength

Prepare yourself for your journey in your usual way.

As you relax the outer world begins to fade then in front of you your old wooden door begins to form. You push the door open and walk through.

The first thing you notice is how warm it is, then looking about you see the scene is a tropical savanna landscape with grasses and small or scattered trees that do not form a closed canopy, allowing sunlight to reach the ground. In the distance you can see a volcano shaped mountain and small groups of animals grazing. Brightly coloured birds flash through the trees their wings making a rainbow of colour. Behind you is a large temple like building of warm glowing stone. From this building a woman walks, she is dressed in a long flowing robe of purest white and draped around her waist and falling toward her feet is a garland of roses which indicate her devotion to a pure and spiritual life. She wears a garland of flowers around her head and above her glows the symbol of life, the endless interweaving circles of the infinity symbol or lemniscate. You are fascinated by her sense of presence and strength. Then over to your left you notice a bush which has suddenly trembled, with a loud roar a large lion comes out from behind the bush and runs towards the woman. She sees it coming and stands quite still. As it approaches she faces it and when it is dangerously close lifts her hand and holds it palm outwards towards the creature. Instantly he stops, gives a final roar, walks gently towards her, then turns and stands at her side. She smiles a welcome, places one hand on his head and the other under his chin, then fondles his magnificent mane. The lion opens his mouth and licks her hand like a great cat. You wonder what kind of magic is this that a lion obeys her will. She gives him a final pat then tells him to go on his way.

So fascinated have you been by this that you have stood frozen to the spot. But you have not gone unnoticed by the lady and she walks over to speak to you. She laughs a little at your astonishment. "Did you think he would harm me?" she asks.

"Yes" you reply.

"I will explain why he obeyed me" she says. "You see when I was young I was very frightened of lions, so much so that I frequently had nightmares where I was walking in the forest and a lion came out of the trees and chased me, I ran for my life and then just as it leaped on my back I awoke, trembling with terror. This happened so often that my parents were concerned and asked a wise friend to talk to me about my dreams. He was so understanding that I had no problem talking to him. He explained that it was wise to be afraid of lions in waking life for they could and would kill one. This he said was nature's way of protecting me and this kind of fear was natural and good. But the dream fear came from some deep level of my mind and the lion represented some unacknowledged fears. In these circumstances it is wise to 'do that which thou fearest and behold thou see'st the end of it' he told me and advised that the next time the dream lion chased me to turn and face him. Of course the dream lion came again and I did as he said and turned to face it, it stopped in its tracks then turned and fled back into the trees. Never again did I dream of the lion chasing me. Then my parents gave me a little orphaned lion cub, he was so tiny and so cute. I reared him and as he grew the bond between us grew deep and strong. He followed me everywhere and learnt to obey my commands. Then of course the time came when he wished to seek his own kind, but every so often he came back to visit me, today was such an occasion. So you see there is no fear between us. But remember fear is your protector when the cause of it is unknown to you. Remember too that the fiercest threat can be tamed with caution by love and trust. If you like I will take you to meet him, he will not harm you if you are with me."

Feeling a little apprehensive you follow the lady, she calls and the Lion appears out of the trees and comes to her. He comes up to her and leans against her leg, she strokes him and invites you to do likewise. With trust in her you gather your strength and approach the lion, he rumbles in a deep voice in his throat but when you stroke his head he calms and accepts you. The three of you stand together for a short time then the lady dismisses the lion and he trots back where he came from.

You thank the lady for giving you this experience then she turns and walks back towards the temple, you too turn and find your entry door forming, you push it open and walk through back into your own time and place.

IX
THE HERMIT.

IX
The Hermit

Prepare for your journey in your usual way.

As you relax the outer world begins to fade then in front of you your old wooden door begins to form. You push the door open and walk through.

You find yourself in a featureless landscape. It is night, the stars shine brightly above you and a full Moon appears partly obscured by clouds. You step into the scene, after walking a little way you notice you are not alone, a tall figure appears before you. He wears a long, hooded robe and carries a staff as tall as himself. He is of mature years and has a full white beard. In his right hand he holds aloft a lantern, within the lantern shines a brilliant star which radiates its illumination around him. He turns to face you and his features are obscured by the darkness. "Greetings Traveller" he says. "I am The Hermit, the inner plane guide to those who are the Way-Showers of humanity. They are those wise souls who descend into incarnation to bring teaching and knowledge to those who seek it. They carry the light for others to follow and become Way-Showers in their turn. I wish to tell you of some of the most notable of these Teachers.

We will start with the Temple knowledge of the ancient land of Egypt and the one known as Hermes Trismegistus. From his teachings came the Hermetic writings which have survived into modern times. Perhaps the most famous is the Emerald Tablet of Hermes Trismegistus which has been translated by several mystics and scholars. It teaches 'as Above so Below', and that creation is One.

Let us talk of the Druids of early times. They were spiritually devoted men and women who underwent lengthy training often lasting more than twenty years. All their knowledge was committed to memory so there were no written records. Like so much esoteric knowledge it went under-ground and continued to influence society for many years.

In legend there was the magician Merlin, which may have been an office held by many rather than a specific person. He is said to have raised and trained Arthur the legendary King. He continues to live in our stories.

In Italy in the twelfth and thirteenth century lived Francis of Assisi, he was the defender of the poor and of the creatures of the animal and bird life. He was one of the first to champion these causes which still struggle for support in modern times.

In Italy also, in the sixteenth century lived Giordano Bruno, he was a Dominican friar who became a student of mysticism and ancient teachings and attempted to have them more widely understood.

He paid the price of being burned as a heretic.

In the sixteenth century also lived John Dee an English mathematician, natural philosopher, and student of mysticism who was involved with the spreading of the ideas of the Enlightenment.

Then in the nineteenth century in India lived Mahatma Gandhi who successfully used non-violence to achieve political ends

These are but a few of the brave souls who taught a spiritual message and changed the ways of the world for the better.

Then there are The Unknown Ones who work tirelessly and silently that the world may learn and become a little better and wiser for their having lived. Before such work may be accomplished for the many each must learn to be master of their own fate, to think for themselves and to be able to be alone. For the work of the Unknown Ones is a solitary path and they must light their own lamp before it can be a beacon to others.

Traveller you have set your foot upon the path and begun the work of the way. I give you a gift to remember me by and so that you may know by its light how to seek me when you are in need." The Hermit steps towards you and places his lamp in your hand. "Travel well." He says, then stepping back he fades into the darkness and you are once more alone.

You spend a little time thinking back on what The Hermit has said to you. Then you lift the lamp in your hand and look about for your door. It slowly appears and you open it and walk through back into your own time and place.

X
T
A
R
O
WHEEL of FORTUNE.

X
Wheel of Fortune

Prepare for your journey in your usual way.

As you relax the outer world begins to fade, then in front of you your old wooden door begins to form. You push the door open and walk through.

You walk forward into a beautiful summer's day and find yourself in a large park. There are trees and lawns surrounding you and colourful flower beds on every side. You walk about exploring what else there may be to see, and as you wander around a corner, there before you is a very large Ferris wheel gently rotating. On its side it carries the symbols of the Four Elements, the Tora and the Yod, He, Vav, He, indicating that it is under the influence of the sacred.

Around the edges of the wheel are three figures which give it momentum and keep it turning gently. They are first, a part human part animal figure which wears a Nemes headdress and who represent the life force, then second a Hermanubis who represents the God Anubis in his role as conductor of souls, and finally the serpent who represents the creative life force. Together they are the forces of life and death which drive the eternal turning of the wheel of life.

The wheel carries twelve carriages in which passengers may ride, each is dedicated to one of the constellations so that each may choose their own birth sign to ride in. Climbing aboard one of the carriages you settle comfortably to enjoy the ride. The wheel begins to turn and depending where you are seated you begin to climb or descend upon the wheel. The scenery below changes and you begin to see events of your own life playing out beneath you. Some are happy and successful while others show you some difficult times in your past. You realise that this is the Wheel of Fortune and that it is showing you that your life is an ever-changing scenario of highs and lows. It is reassuring that even as you descend the curve of the wheel you are approaching the ascent, and that you reach the peak only to begin the descent again. Round and round you go on the wheel and you see that the other eleven carriages carry others who are, likewise, reliving the highs and lows of their lives - for this is what life is for everyone. Because the Wheel of Life is constantly revolving everything in life is constantly changing, to see life as settled and unchanging is an illusion. The events in the lives of others all have an influence on our own, these may be fortunate or unfortunate according to our point of view. Every turn of the wheel builds a different pattern and every event builds the karma of our lives from this to the next in an eternal dance of fortune.

As you look down the view changes, no longer the scenes of your life, you look at the world beneath you and gradually you seem to go higher and higher, the Earth receding in your view until you are looking down on the north pole, the ice fields reflecting the sunlight and the whole planet revolving before your eyes. The view expands and you see the sun, itself revolving and the other planets spinning around it. The stars of our galaxy revolving too, until we see our whole galaxy in a mighty panorama revolving about the black hole at its centre. This is our Wheel of Fortune spinning in space. At the furthest corners of the heavens we see the mighty Watchers of the Heavens. In the constellation of Aquarius stands the Winged Man, ruler of the element of Air in the image of mighty archangel Raphael. In the constellation of Scorpio is the Eagle, ruler of the element of Water in the image of mighty archangel Gabriel. In the constellation of Leo is the Winger Lion, ruler of the element of Fire in the image of the mighty archangel Michael. In the constellation of Taurus is the Winged Bull, ruler of the element of Earth in the image of the mighty archangel Uriel. They stand guard over our Universe, watching our progress, our victories, and failures. They do not interfere in our activities for to do so would negate our free will. But they are there for us in our need when we ask for their help, as ask we must to enable this help.

Gradually we descend until we are once more within Earth's atmosphere and the clouds hide the Watchers from our view, but we know they are ever present watching over us.

We are once more aware of the carriage of the wheel that we have been riding in and it allows us to descend and we are back on the grass of the garden. We begin to walk towards the trees and flower beds when gradually our door forms in front of us and we walk through back into our own time and place.

XI
JUSTICE.

XI
Justice

Prepare for your journey in your usual way.

As you relax the outer world begins to fade, then in front of you your old wooden door begins to form. You push the door open and walk through.

You find yourself standing in a crowd of people lining the pavement outside a magnificent cathedral like building. There is a buzz of excitement in the air and you wonder what you are all waiting for. Then, your question is answered as you see a procession coming towards you in the roadway between the two banks of people on either side. They come two by two in a long column, men and women both. They are dressed in the long scarlet robes and wigs of the judiciary of the nation. A gentleman beside you tells you that this is the annual meeting of the Judges of the nation. It is these men and women who maintain the rule of law, they administer justice within the framework of the law of the land. This is a human made set of laws and as such is fallible. Justice is not always served in their decisions. But they serve a necessary purpose. Their office gives them considerable status and power within the community.

The last pair disappear through the large doorway and those who wish are allowed to follow them in. You enter and find yourself in a magnificent building, the procession has reached the end of the aisle and they are seating themselves. You too find a seat. The High Priest enters accompanied by a procession of assistants and the choir. They take their places and the ceremony begins. It is a service of blessing of the work of the Judges, it is asked that the higher Powers may assist them in their decisions and that they may be blessed with wisdom in their work. It is only a short ceremony, it is soon over and the Judges and their procession reform and leave. You too follow them back into the outer world.

But instead of finding yourself back in the street, before you there is another stately building, the street around it is deserted. You approach the large doorway and enter the building. Inside you find yourself looking at a large circular hall. Around its circumference are a series of identical carved wooden chairs with scarlet cushions. A bell chimes and one by one a line of white robed figures enter and slowly perambulate around the circle before each stops at their own seat.

You count them and recognise them as the Forty Two Assessors of the Ancient Egyptian Tradition. You realise they are of a higher level than the Judges and that it is a person's integrity that they are here to judge. An attendant indicates that you should walk clockwise around the circle stopping at each of the Assessors as you do so. With some trepidation you obey and go to the first and receive their question, replying to each one in the Truth of Maat.

1. Hast thou given due thought to the body inhabited by thee?
2. Hast thou lived the fullness of time allotted to thee?
3. Hast thou refrained from being unclean in body and mind?

4. Hast thou loved with the body, only where the heart is also?
5. Hast thou had knowledge forbidden to thee?
6. Hast thou kept thee only to the sword or distaff?
7. Hast thou respected the bodies of the younger brethren?
8. Hast thou stolen?
9. Hast thou taken food and drink to excess?
10. Hast thou killed?
11. Hast thou spoken unjustly in anger?
12. Hast thou looked upon the goods of others in envy?
13. Hast thou known jealously?
14. Hast thou spoken ill of any man or woman in anger?
15. Hast thou been un-diligent in work?
16. Hast thou profaned the mysteries?
17. Hast thou known pride in thyself that is false?
18. Hast thou strayed from the path allotted thee?
19. Hast thou lusted for precious metals?
20. Hast thou been too worldly?
21. Hast thou been just in thy dealings in the market place?
22. Hast thou repaid all debts promptly?
23. Hast thou been generous to the needy?
24. Hast thou lied to gain from others?
25. Hast thy tongue been as a viper to cause laughter in others?
26. Hast thou been a friend?

27. Hast thou hated another to the exclusion of all else?
28. Hast thou lent thy body to any from the other side?
29. Hast thou been thy parent's joy?
30. Hast thou honoured all faiths that are of the light?
31. Hast thou given time to be at peace with the gods?
32. Hast thou turned aside from wisdom given in love?
33. Hast thou listened to that which is not for thy ears?
34. Hast thou lived in the light?
35. Hast thou been a sword for the weak?
36. Hast thou enslaved any other life?
37. Hast thou faced the mirror of self?
38. Hast thou taken the words of his mouth from any man as thine own?
39. Hast thou known that all journeys end but to begin?
40. Hast thou remembered the brethren of the Earth, and been compassionate to those younger brethren who serve thee as beasts in the field and home?
41. Hast thou ever worked man or beast beyond its strength in greed?
42. Is there one upon the Earth who is glad thou hast lived?

Feeling sobered and humbled you exit the circle to be met by the first assessor who has risen from their place to stand beside you and leaning forward says quietly to you "Since we are all human we none of us are without fault. But it is not the fact of our guilt or innocence which matters, it is the knowing of oneself and being able to answer in honesty and truth. Go onward knowing that there are many voices raised in gladness that thou hast lived."

You leave the hall to find that it is now evening and the first stars are shining against the darkness of the evening sky. You wander around the building and find a quiet park to the rear. There is a small altar decorated with flowers and you pause in front of it. Then in the sky a few feet above ground level a vision begins to form. It does not have any support but floats in the air. You see a woman seated on a throne like chair, she wears a flowing red gown with very full sleeves and draped over her shoulders a golden cloak. About her neck is the stole of her office. She sits between two pillars whose names are Balance and Law. In her right hand she holds aloft a large sword which she looks very capable of using. You know that this sword destroys what is out of balance and calls us to account for our actions. It indicates that our actions always carry consequences for which we are responsible. The sword also presents the choice of staying as we are or adopting real action to change. In her left hand she holds a set of golden scales, perfectly balanced, these symbolise the balance between good and bad and that there is always justice, equality and fairness between them. We recognise that the Lady represent Justice at a cosmic level, however it may appear at our worldly level, Justice always prevails, there is a law in the Universe which maintains the balance.

The unspoken message which the Lady conveys to you begins to fade away. Then you notice the park is fading and in its place your doorway is forming. You approach the door and walk through it back into your own time and place.

XII
THE HANGED MAN.

XII
The Hanged Man

Prepare for your journey in your usual way.

As you relax the outer world begins to fade, then in front of you your old wooden door begins to form. You push the door open and walk through.

You find yourself in a sunny meadow with a small stream running on your left-hand side. You walk beside the stream for some distance before realising that there is a low hill to your right-hand side, it is grassy and easy to walk up which you begin to do. Then you notice that there is something on the top of the hill. As you get closer you see it is a tree with a branch growing out on either side of the top forming it into a Tau cross with green branches growing out from it. This is the ancient form of the cross, sacred in ancient Babylon to the Sumerian Sun God Tammuz, God of death and resurrection. It was used in Ancient Egypt representing the Sacred Opening, or portal. In Rome it symbolised the god Mithras and in Greece the god Attis. It was the earliest form of the cross in Christianity, being most famous as the favourite symbol of St Francis of Assisi. In all traditions it is and has been the symbol of immortality.

As you ponder the meaning of the Tau cross you observe a figure suspended by his right ankle from the top of it, His left knee is bent so that his left leg forms a triangle with his body and his arms are folded behind his back. His head is surrounded by a golden nimbus and his face is suffused with the same golden glow. It is as if his head is the Sun of his being radiating the light of his life force. As you watch him you get the feeling that he too has noticed you. Then with a quick twist of his body he straightens his left leg and shakes his right foot free, then so fast you almost think it was illusion, he somersaults off the tree and lands on his feet before you. He smiles at you and says "Hello" as if you were old friends. You take a closer look at him, then he says, "I am the Fool."

"Well so you are" you say.

He continues "Like you I am only visiting this level this time, having left my body in the material world. I was connecting with the universal Life Force which flows through the Cross of the Tree. Every living being, human, animal, bird, insect, tree, plant or fish to the smallest plankton of the oceans, is animated by the same Life Force. It is an energy just as are light or electricity, it animates a vehicle for its life span then flows on to the next. One of the faculties of the Life Force is that it carries consciousness from vehicle to vehicle and in the process it grows and develops. It is the purpose of the incarnating Life Force to learn and develop so that it may in the fullness of time become worthy of blending with the Great Cosmic Mind of the Universe. There are sources within the Cosmos which radiate the Life Force as the Sun radiates physical light, even so on a lesser level does my life force radiate this Life Light which you see as the nimbus around my head. As above so below. These lights are of different wavelengths yet All Light is One. This is the mystery of the Mystery."

"Why are you called The Fool when you are so wise" you say.

He grins at you and says "Do you not know that the best place to conceal a secret is in full sight? Even so does The Fool conceal knowledge and wisdom in his foolishness? I am also The Hanged Man who by my viewpoint can see into both the inner and the outer worlds. I am not a sacrifice but a messenger, reverse your viewpoint and you too will see. Goodbye." With this he skips away and fades from sight.

You watch the tree for a while wondering if he will reappear there, but he does not and you realise it is time for you to return to your own level. The desire is enough to make your door appear, when it does you step through back into your own time and place.

XIII
DEATH.

XIII
Death

Prepare for your journey in your usual way.

As you relax the outer world begins to fade, then in front of you your old wooden door begins to form. You push the door open and walk through.

You find yourself standing by a large window in what looks like an office room, the window looks down from the first floor onto a wide thoroughfare stretching away between tall buildings. The street is lined with rows of people on either side, they are all silent and solemn. From your right-hand side there appears a procession, leading it is a military band, but the only sound from them is the slow beating of drums, after this are ranks of service men and women and members of government. Then there is a space, followed by a large white horse ridden by a figure in ornamental ceremonial black armour. He carries a black banner which bears a large symbolic white rose, symbolising purity and spiritual rebirth. He wears a skull mask, symbolising death of the body. Behind him on a ceremonial gun carriage comes a coffin laid on the flag of the country and on the top of the coffin is a splendid crown. A long procession of mourners follows.

As you watch the procession you become aware of someone beside you and turn to see The Hermit. "Greetings" he says, "I have come to guide you through the experience of this card. What you see before you is the state funeral of the ruler of a country. He had absolute power in his hands and had great wealth at his disposal. He lacked for nothing in worldly power or influence. He was only of middle years and thought nothing could touch him. Yet a sickness that none could mend overtook him and he succumbed to the summons of Death. Even so are the great of this world forced to learn that they are not immune and all are subject to the rule of Death. Popes and Bishops, Emperors and Kings, the wealthy and the powerful, even as the poor and the beggar, all must obey when He calls." You ponder for a while on the inevitability of death for all that lives, it is an inescapable end to life. "That is true." says The Hermit. "Yet for some it is welcome. When the body has become a burden from age or disease the soul discards it and flows again in the vast sea of the Life Force. Even an infant who meets death before life is set free to seek a healthier vehicle. When we are of the living we grieve to be separated from our loved ones but should not begrudge them their freedom."

The procession fades into the distance. "Come let us explore the journey." says The Hermit.

The scene beyond the window fades and changes and you are looking down on a battlefield. The battle is over and the living are leaving the field, there are many dead and dying and you watch as their spirit's Life Force breaks free of the bodies and disappears as they are absorbed into an energy field you cannot observe. The Hermit too observes the scene then says "This is death inflicted on men by men. It has ever been so in human conflicts. Even as you are the cause, so too do you have the cure in your own hands." The scene changes again. The Hermit shows you many forms of death, from the elderly leaving outworn bodies to those killed by the carelessness or wickedness of others. Then he changes his theme and begins to speak of the many ideas of what happens after death that humans have suggested over the centuries. One of the oldest is the idea that there is a river called the Styx which has to be crossed. It is wide and fast flowing and there is no way to cross it, except by a small boat which appears with a boatman called Charon, who asks for a coin to take the soul across. Hence the custom of placing a coin in the hand of the dying with which to pay the Ferryman.

Whatever the means of crossing the divide between the place of the living and that of the dead, there is always a pathway which leads to two pillars which mark the entrance to a world of Light. Between the pillars radiates the sun of the Life Force which shines on the fields of immortality.

You turn and The Hermit is no longer with you, darkness hides the world beyond the window and you realise this journey is at an end. Your door begins to form in front of you and you walk through back into your own time and place.

XIV
TEMPERANCE.

XIV
Temperance

Prepare for your journey in your usual way.

As you relax the outer world begins to fade, then in front of you your old wooden door begins to form. You push the door open and walk through.

You find yourself on a seashore, the sands stretching away on either hand, the sea has a gentle swell and the tide is almost full in. The land is composed of high sand dunes with here and there patches of fertile land meeting the sea. On one of these grows white Iris, symbolising hope, wisdom, and courage. You stroll along the beach enjoying the scenery, pausing now and then to paddle your feet in the sea. You have paused for a while deep in thought when you become aware of someone standing at your shoulder, you turn and see a woman of middle years and handsome countenance. She is wearing a long flowing robe of shining white, she greets you and introduces herself saying, "Hello, I have come to be your guide. My name is Mnemosyne, and I was considered one of the goddesses in Ancient Greece. I hold the keys to your memories and will help you to recall them."

You continue your walk together for a while then Mnemosyne pauses and takes your arm to draw your attention. Pointing towards one of the clumps of Iris she says, "Watch, for an angel is coming to share knowledge with you." You look towards the land and see nothing at first, then slowly a figure begins to form. First you see a human form, the face is delicate and neither male nor yet female but a delicate blend of both. The figure is standing one foot on the dry land and the other in the sea where it has reached high tide for she exists in both elements. She wears a long white robe, on its neckline are embroidered the Yod He Vav He of the Holy Name showing her as belonging to the Divine, and on her breast the triangle in the square signifying the holy Earth and the fire which animates it. Behind her, rising from her shoulders, are two mighty wings, one on each side, symbolising her role as a messenger of the Divine. On her forehead she wears the symbol of the Sun and around her head shines the nimbus of the Life Force. In each hand she holds a chalice and is pouring water from one to the other and back again. Mnemosyne explains she is pouring the life of the physical and the life of the spiritual, so that they constantly flow one into the other.

Then she says that the figure is also Time and she is showing how the past and the present constantly flow into each other. Mnemosyne says that she wishes to explain time and continues. "Time as it is known on Earth to humans is an illusion which is created by the motions of the heavens, for a day is but one revolution of the Earth as it circles to face the Sun and a year one revolution of the Earth around the Sun. But the point of the present is ever in the same place on the Earth as it circles. For the past exists only in memory and the future in imagination. The present is the consciousness of the Now and we move with it constantly, as one moment flows into the next we move with it. Yet Time also signifies change, everything in the Now is constantly changing, growing to maturity and then changing and ageing. The angel is demonstrating the balance that exists in creation between physical and spiritual life, everything in the Now works in accordance with the eternal Laws of the Cosmos."

Mnemosyne then draws your attention to a pathway which seems to emerge from the sea onto the land, you follow it with your eyes as it follows the slowly rising land. Until at last it begins to climb the distant mountains, first the foothills then the high mountains beyond. Then in the sky you see a radiant golden crown surrounded by a nimbus of golden light, it is dazzling in its splendour. Mnemosyne tells you that this is the goal of all your days in the Now, that when you reach the summit of the mountains she will hand you the keys to all you have learnt about on your journey. The Angel Time and Balance begins to fade in front of your eyes until only the scene of the sea and land remain. Mnemosyne takes your hand and tells you that she must leave you and then she too fades away.

You continue to walk along the beach, sometimes walking in the sea as the tide turns and begins to flow out. Then you too feel the pull of your own place and at that thought your doorway forms in front of you and you walk through back into your own time and place.

XV
THE DEVIL.

XV
The Devil

Prepare for your journey in your usual way.

As you relax the outer world begins to fade, then in front of you your old wooden door begins to form. You push the door open and walk through.

You find yourself walking down a long corridor and at its end are a pair of very imposing doors. They are of beautifully carved wood, light in colour, with matching columns on either side and gold doorknobs on each door. You hesitate, wondering if you would be intruding if you opened the doors. "You are welcome to enter" says a voice behind you. You turn and see The Hermit standing there. You had not heard him following you down the corridor. You greet him with pleasure at his presence and ask why he is here. He tells you that he is here to accompany you and to explain what you will see beyond the doors. He tells you that you are about to enter the Hall of the Gods. A title which fills you with some trepidation and a gratitude for his presence.

Following his instruction you go forward and take hold of one of the doorknobs and open the door. The sight which meets your eyes is of a very long hall, wider than it first appears because of its length. The lighting is soft and low but bright enough for you to distinguish details. On either side of the hall hang opposing rows of what you at first take to be pictures. You go to stand in front of the first in the row to your left, accompanied by The Hermit. At first you see nothing then you see a notice across the bottom which reads 'early stone age goddess' you read this out loud and as you do so an image begins to form. It is a rather crude statue of a seated woman about to give birth. The Hermit explains "These are not paintings but a kind of magical mirror which reflects the mind images of the people who worshipped the gods and goddesses you will see in the mirrors. For the gods and goddesses of a people are images which are constructed by their worshipers. They do not reflect the true appearance of The Divine but are images built by humans. It is through the agency of these images that the Divine may communicate with the souls of humanity. Let us move on."

The next mirror is labelled 'The Creator God of the Egyptians' and you recognise the image of Atum. Walking on past the next few mirrors you see first Osiris, then Isis and several more of the Egyptian pantheon. The next mirrors move on to the many Gods and Goddesses of Ancient Greece, prime among them being Zeus. Then we come to their Roman counterparts with first amongst them being Jupiter followed by the many gods and goddesses he rules. The next mirror shows a large golden Sun with a radiating aura, this is Sol Invictus, the Unconquered Sun. Then there is a mirror with the more familiar figures of our culture, here is Jesus and his Mother Mary.

A shock then rushes through you as you face the next figure. This is not an appealing one, he bears the label The Devil. Before you in the mirror is a large, bearded figure, half man half beast, he is winged and horned and upon his brow is a large, inverted pentagram. In his left hand he holds an immense flaming torch. He is perched on a black double cube altar. On either side at his feet stand two figures, a man and a woman, both of whom are horned and tailed. The woman's tail ends in a bunch of grapes and the man's in the colour of fire as if it has been heated from the flaming torch. The couple stand one on either side of the altar and about their necks are large chains which bind them to a ring on the front of the altar. It is obvious that these chains are loose about their necks and could quite easily be removed should they so wish. They appear to be small demons who are in servitude to The Devil yet they only need to raise their hands and remove the chains to be free, they remain chained of their own free will. Just as the figures of the Gods and Goddesses are reflections of human thought so too is The Devil, he does not inflict evil upon humans but is built from their thoughts and acts which have evil and painful effects in the world. It is human belief which gives power to the images.

The Hermit tells you that each image has significance for you and to look within yourself for the source of their power. Then he turns away and continues to the next mirror.

The Hermit leads you past the next few mirrors which he says depict the same thought forms as The Devil. Here is Angra Mainyu of the Zorastrians, T'an-mo of the Chinese, Set of the Egyptians, O-Yama of the Japanese, Loki of the Teutonic, Lileth of the Hebrew and several more. Then you come back to the gods and goddesses and wise teachers such as Hermes Trismegistus, Buddha, Confucius, Mohammed and Jesus. You wander from mirror to mirror absorbing the power and beauty which has been built into the images over the centuries.

At last you find yourself back at the doors by which you entered the hall, you turn to speak to The Hermit but he has disappeared and when you turn around to face the doors you see they have dissolved and changed into your own door, you open it and pass back into your own time and place.

XVI
THE TOWER.

XVI
The Tower

Prepare for your journey in your usual way.

As you relax the outer world begins to fade, then in front of you your old wooden door begins to form. You push the door open and walk through.

You find yourself walking into a beautiful parkland. About you are immaculate green lawns with many trees of different varieties, here and there flower beds full of flowers of glowing colours shine out. In the distance you can see a magnificent mansion house and some distance from that, built on a small rock, is a tall tower. There are several windows built at different levels and the whole is surmounted by what looks like a semi-circular roof decorated to look like a golden crown. You notice someone working at one of the flower beds who looks like a gardener, you walk over to him and greet him. You ask him who lives in the mansion and if it is alright for you to be walking in the park. He says the lord of the mansion likes people to admire his estate.

He tells you that the lord is a high official in the kingdom and very wealthy. He draws your attention to the tower and says that its construction was the result of a competition between the lord and another high official who competed with him for the attention of the King. It was the result of their vanity and ambition. The two had vied with each other to build the tallest, most lavish, and most impressive tower. You ask if it is possible to see the inside of the tower and to climb it to see the view. The gardener says yes it would normally be possible but not today as the King is there on a private visit and the tower is closed to other visitors. The gardener says it is the Kings first visit and the noble is very hopeful that he will be impressed by the tower and that it will improve his status in the kingdom.

The two of you chat for a while when you notice that the sky is darkening, heavy clouds are gradually filling the sky. You realise that there is going to be a heavy storm and it would be wise to seek shelter. The gardener shows you the way to a sturdy summer house and you both stand in the doorway watching the approaching storm. The clouds get thicker and the sky darker and suddenly the storm breaks and a mighty downpour of rain comes crashing down. You retreat into the summer house and continue to watch through the windows. All at once there is a mighty flash of lightning followed by a massive crash of thunder and to your horror you see that the tower has been struck. So powerful was the impact that the entire top of the tower has been sliced off and the crown like roof is falling through the air. You are appalled to see the King and the Noble have been thrown off the tower where they must have been on the very top balcony. They are falling through the air headfirst towards the ground. You notice there are also several people falling from the windows. In the sky around them are a number of Yod shaped flames, indicating that this is a celestial power at work. You are horrified by the fate of these falling people then as suddenly as the lightning struck, there is another flash and the whole scene vanishes from your sight and the tower stands unharmed before you.

You realise that this was a prophetic vision and there is still time to warn the King and his company. You wonder if they will listen to you since you have no status or power in this kingdom or will they just dismiss you as foolish. You ponder on the fact that disaster can overtake any one of us, no matter how powerful we may be in a worldly sense, at any time and without warning. It is telling us that nothing in life is permanent or guaranteed, even life itself.

You turn to the gardener and thank him for his company and tell him what you have seen and that you will seek an audience with the Noble or the King and tell them of your vision. He says he doubts if they will grant you an audience on such a mission. You say that you can only try and then bid him farewell.

You part company and you begin to walk back the way you came until you see the outer wall of the park and in it your door waiting for you, it is a welcome sight, and you go to it and walk through back into your own time and place.

XVII
THE STAR.

XVII
The Star

Prepare for your journey in your usual way.

As you relax the outer world begins to fade, then in front of you your old wooden door begins to form. You push the door open and walk through.

On the inner side of the door you find yourself in the darkness of night with just sufficient glow to see that you are standing on top of a hill. It feels familiar, then you notice there is what looks like a church tower rising from the top of the hill, you recognise it and realise you are standing by Saint Michael's tower at the summit of Glastonbury Tor. The landscape below you is lost in the darkness, but above you blazes the panorama of the stars.

The sky is filled with the majesty of the Milky Way of our galaxy and the innumerable galaxies and their stars which surround us. You look upwards to locate the Polar Star around which the Universe appears to rotate, then find the constellation Ursa Major and follow it to locate the constellation of Orion. The three stars of the belt of Orion lead you to the brightest star in the night sky, mighty Sirius. This is the closest star to our own Sun and bigger and brighter than most others, it is a binary star, being composed of two stars which orbit each other. It is now thought there is a third small but very dense and powerful star which orbits with the other two. The fact that light travels to Earth and enables us to see all these other celestial bodies says that other radiations must also do so. We live in a sea of radiating energy both visible and invisible to our eyes. Sirius streams out these energies which spread their influence over us just as the energies of the Moon do. Traditionally the influence of Sirius is on nature and its flourishing, also on inspiration and blessings of the universe. It is also traditionally responsible for the continuity of water; clouds, the seas, rain, rivers, lakes and of evaporation which returns the water once more to the clouds and the ever repeating cycle.

The rising of Sirius in Ancient Egypt signalled the flooding of the Nile and the repeating cycles of fertility of the Nile valley. In Ancient Greece its rising signalled the Dog Days of summer which is why it is often known as the Dog Star.

Sirius is also associated with baptism and redemption, both strongly associated with water. A few drops of rain remind you where you are and you gaze once more into the night sky, you feel the pull of Sirius and find yourself rising into the sky. You do not need wings for it is your consciousness which rises and you are only aware of being. You feel as if you are riding on a wave of power between Sirius and Earth.

After a time your view focusses on Earth and you see our beautiful blue planet far below, you realise that it is because of the size of the seas that the Earth looks blue. Then your viewpoint changes again, the figure of a beautiful naked woman forms in front of you, she smiles at you and tells you she is the Goddess of Water and oversees all the forms of water on Earth, from ice and snow, to steam and vapour, to fluid water. She sends you welcoming thoughts and bids you return to Earth with her so that she may demonstrate her functions to you. With that you find yourself standing beside a wide river and kneeling beside it is the Goddess, one foot in the water and the other on the land. She holds a large jug in either hand and is pouring water from them, one into the river and the other on the land where all about her nature flourishes. You realise She is the power which keeps the fertility of land and sea flourishing.

The vision fades and you find yourself back on Glastonbury Tor. The stars are growing dimmer and the first flush of dawn is just touching the eastern sky. There is a light rain falling and you turn to see if you can take shelter in the tower. As you approach seeking a doorway you find there is no way into the tower, then one appears and you recognise your own door and go through it back into your own time and place.

XVIII
THE MOON.

XVIII
The Moon

Prepare for your journey in your usual way.

As you relax the outer world begins to fade, then in front of you your old wooden door begins to form. You push the door open and walk through.

It is dark on the other side and it takes you a few moments to realise where you are. Feeling a slight swaying motion you discern that you are seated in a small boat which rocks gently on the surface of the sea. There is a small sail which is guiding you along. It is night but the sky is lit with a full moon which shines directly ahead of you, it is so bright that it is masking the presence of some of the stars. The reflection of the Moon is glistening on the surface of the sea and creating a kind of pathway down which your boat is sailing towards the shore, which you eventually reach and the boat beaches itself gently.

As you prepare to step out onto the land you notice a crayfish climbing out of the water. You remember that the crayfish is a symbol of regeneration since it can lose its claws and regrow them. He is heading towards a stream which flows down to the shore from the hills some distance away. On the left side of the stream is a dog, and on the right a fox-like creature, who are baying towards a large full moon in the sky before you. You realise that the sea has brought you to an inner landscape, for the sea is symbolic of the deep levels of your psyche and here you may meet with your dreams and intuitions. This is the realm of the subconscious which holds all your memories including those which you cannot consciously recall.

The dog and the fox are guardians of these deep levels of the mind. They are baying at a large full Moon which reflects the light of the Sun into the night sky of Earth. The Moon appears to hang in the sky between two tall towers which stand on the foothills in the landscape. These mark the limits to the south and to the north, of the path of the Moon as it orbits Earth. The dance of the Moon around the Earth as they orbit the Sun together, and the gravitational forces which hold them together, have powerful effects upon Earth. They govern the tides of the seas with such precision that they can be charted years in advance. All living things on Earth, including humans, are influenced by the Moon's energies. They influence growth and cyclic patterns in all life.

By this time you have climbed out of the boat and are walking towards the two towers; the dog and fox give you suspicious looks and sniff the air enquiringly. Something in you recognises what they truly represent and you understand that they are part of your own animal nature. You pause and look up towards the Moon and for the first time you see that there is a female face drawn on its surface and there are bright rays surrounding it which shine on to the Earth beneath. Then as you watch the face changes, it moves and seems to become alive, it is as if a living woman looks out at you, as though she were looking out of a window between her world and yours. She is very beautiful and her long golden hair wraps about her. She smiles at you then introduces herself. "Hello, I am Selene" she says "welcome to my realm. You have been here many times but do not remember, but this time you are awake and I will gift you with memory. Every night you swim in the sea of sleep and dreams, which sometimes teach you of the inner worlds and sometimes are just a nonsense sorting of your mundane mind, which rises from your subconscious. I am the light which shines on the pathways of night, mine are the ways of intuition which prompts with knowledge to instruct your future days. Mine are the ways of mystery and romance which draw one to another. My turning measures the days and nights of time and the ever-changing panoply of your lives. I govern the ebbing and flowing of the tides of the great seas and the life forms which dwell therein. I take the hand of those who seek knowledge of the spiritual worlds and teach them in dream and symbol. Remember that my light is the reflection of that greater Light which shines from your Sun. Know that all Light is one. As the inner and the outer, the above and below are one, even so are outer and inner Light One. Come to me in your seeking and I will bless you, guide you and teach you. Farewell Seeker until we meet again in dream."

So saying a dark cloud comes over the Moon and Selene disappears from your view.

You feel that your time here is drawing to a close and you turn and walk back towards the sea. Your boat awaits you and you climb aboard and sitting down feel the boat begin to move out onto the surface of the sea. The gentle motion of the sea lulls you almost into sleep and then you rouse to find you have passed through your door and are back in your own time and place.

XIX
THE SUN .

XIX
The Sun

Prepare for your journey in your usual way.

As you relax the outer world begins to fade, then in front of you your old wooden door begins to form. You push the door open and walk through.

When you pass through your door you feel slightly weightless and peculiar, then you come to realise that you are out of your physical body and floating in your astral body in the deep blue of the sky. You rise higher and higher in the sky until you can see the Earth below you. Higher you go until you are looking down on the Sun and can see all the planets circling it. It is a dazzling sight, with our own Earth having a slight blue tinge to the light appearing to shine from it. You realise that none of the planets, including Earth, shine with light of its own but with the reflected light of the Sun. In the background gleam all the multitude of stars of the distant galaxies. As you gaze on the Sun and its circling planets you realise what a compact little family we make amidst the vast distances of our nearest neighbours. You think about how none of our brother and sister planets bear any life forms and what a miracle our little home is. Your heart fills with love for our planet and a prayer rises in you that humanity will awaken to the beauty of it and our need to care for it. You appear to rise still higher until you are looking down at the Sun and watch as it rotates and you realise that all in the vast cosmos is moving.

All around you shine other stars of our galaxy and you consider the amazing fact that the galaxy of the

Milky Way, with our Sun and its planets, are all on a gigantic orbit around the galactic centre, which takes it approximately 240 million years to complete. Descending nearer to the Sun you drift down a sunbeam and find yourself back on Earth with the Sun shining brightly above you.

You are stood in front of a beautiful garden but you cannot see a way into it because it is surrounded by a high wall with tall sunflowers rising over the top. Perhaps this is a private garden or a sacred realm you are not ready to enter. You hear a trotting and coming towards you is a white horse on which rides a small child, completely naked except for a crown of flowers. He carries a scarlet banner, swirling in the breeze, which proclaims his victory over life and death. He is humanity rising over the challenges of life and he is proclaiming his joy at connecting with the inner spirit. For he has discovered that life is a stage of development and death is but a transformation to the next stage. Life flows in a continuous stream like his banner, death is but the discarding of an outworn body so that the immortal consciousness can move on to a new one.

Beyond the wall shines the Sun, its rays flooding down to bring life and fertility to the Earth. This is our parent, for every particle of Earth, the landmasses, the growing things, the animals and humanity, they are all children of the Sun. Every atom had its birth in that fiery cauldron.

You look up towards the Sun and think you see the form of a face looking back at you from its surface. Then as you look it becomes a single great eye with a brilliant nimbus surrounding it which appears to gaze down on you. This is said to be the Eye of God watching over the world in beneficence and guardianship. It is a symbol of the spiritual progress of humanity, of its journey to learn independence of thought and understanding of the laws which govern the working of the inner and the outer worlds. It is a symbol of those who can say "I of my own knowledge tell you that this is so." For only when we have learnt through our own experience, and not through the words of others, can we truly speak in truth.

Throughout the ages humanity has venerated the Sun and often worshipped it as a god under many names. It is indeed the star of our existence and worthy of our reverence. Sol Invictus. The light which shines from the Sun illuminates both our material physical world and our inner spiritual world, but in a different manner. For as St John said, "and the light shineth in darkness; and the darkness comprehended it not." For we are in darkness to the spiritual light until our inner eye opens to it. St John also said, "That was the true Light, which lighteth every man that cometh into the world." Yet all Light is one. So shall we know it to be when the Great Work is accomplished.

The great Eye of the Sun fades from view and you realise that it is time to return to your own time and place, you look about for your door and see it form in front of you, you push it open and walk through to find yourself back in your physical reality.

XX
JUDGEMENT.

XX
Judgement

Prepare for your journey in your usual way.

As you relax the outer world begins to fade, then in front of you your old wooden door begins to form. You push the door open and walk through.

The world you find yourself in is like a mirror image of the material world, it feels almost like your familiar physical world but you know it is not, it is more like a very vivid dream. This tells you that you are on the astral plane.

You are standing on a seashore with the sea lapping at your feet. The sea is almost on the full tide and the waves are high and topped with white foam, they crash spectacularly on to the backwash of the tide as it pulls back from the shore. You notice what at first appears to be debris washing up the beach, but you realise that they are coffins which are becoming lodged on the sand. You wonder if they come from some catastrophe and begin to walk over to them to investigate. To your horror you see that the lids are open and inside lie two groups of a man, woman and child. A sound catches your attention, looking upwards you see the head and shoulders of a mighty winged figure. From the fact that he is upheld by clouds and wears a crown of clouds you think he may be Raphael, the mighty archangel of air, whose function it is to give us comfort, guidance, and protection as we journey through the stages of our lives. In his hands he holds a silver and gold trumpet from which hangs a square banner bearing a red cross, which is internationally identified with those who give humanitarian aid to anyone in need, without discrimination of race or creed.

Without warning he begins to sound the trumpet and as the sounds ring out your attention is called once more towards the coffins. You watch fascinated as a cloudy column rises from each one and gradually forms into the shapes of men, women and children who stretch out their arms towards the Angel. The people sing out in joy and as the Angel continues to play they rise up towards him. Ceasing to play as they reach him, he stretches out his arms in welcome to them. They all begin to rise towards the sky, led by the Angel. As they do so their apparent forms slowly dissolve and they pass from your view. You realise that what you thought were dead bodies are really still alive and journeying with the Angel. You walk over to the coffins and discover they are not empty but within them lie the discarded bodies of the souls you have just witnessed departing with the Angel. For soul energy inhabits bodies, be they human, animal or plant and death is a normal and inevitable consequence of life. With death of physical form soul energy is released back into its divine cosmic source.

Thinking on these things you become aware again of the sea, its breakers still rolling in towards you. This is an inner sea and therefore symbolic of the deeper subconscious levels of your mind and you allow some ideas and thought to rise to consciousness and dwell upon them,

You think of the miracle of nature that enables each species to reproduce their kind, which they have been doing over the millenniums. Life is an incredible gift and while it can be hard at times, to expand one's viewpoint to look at the wonder of this oasis of life in the vast Universe, is to cheer our spirits and enjoy it.

You feel it is time for your return and look about you for your door, at the thought it forms in front of you and you open it and pass though into your own time and place.

XXI
THE WORLD.

XXI
The World

Prepare for your journey in your usual way.

As you relax the outer world begins to fade, then in front of you your old wooden door begins to form. You push the door open and walk through.

It is night-time that you step into, and you find yourself standing on the top of a mound in the middle of a meadow. It is one of the special places designated as Dark Sky Discovery areas where there is the least light pollution and the best view of the stars. The sky is filled with a brilliant display of the constellations and the Milky Way.

You decide to look for the four Guardians of the Heavens and begin to locate their constellations.

First you find Aquarius and its major star Formalhaut shining brilliantly against the dark background. This star represents The Winged Man of the four Holy Creatures and Raphael of the four great Archangels.

Next you look for Scorpio and its major star Antares, known as the Heart of the Scorpion, again remarkable for its brilliance. This star represents The Eagle of the four Holy Creatures and Gabriel of the four great Archangels,

Then you look for Leo and its vivid major star Regulus known as the Lion's Heart which represents the Winged Lion of the Holy Creatures and Michael of the four great Archangels.

Finally you seek Taurus and its brilliant major star Aldebaran, which is known as the Eye of the Bull and represents the Bull of the Holy Creatures and Uriel of the four great Archangels.

These are the four fixed signs of the Zodiac and represent the four quarters of the Universe. The Four Holy Creatures are the guardians over the creatures of Earth, the Winged Man over humanity, the Eagle over birds, the Winged Lion over wild animals, and the Bull over domesticated animals.

You observe that the light from the four stars is getting brighter and, as though they are riding on the beams, the Four Holy Creatures come sliding down the Light, gradually assuming their Archangel forms until they stand in a square before you.

A very large laurel wreath has formed in the centre of the square and a young woman comes dancing into the square and leaps through the laurel wreath, the symbol of victory. Around her is draped a banner of life such as the Child of the Sun wore, and in each hand she carries a wand, showing that she can command the powers she has been learning from her Tarot journey. Her name is Sophia, because she is Wisdom Incarnate. She dances to celebrate her completion of the Great Work, the goal of the mystical seeker. In the background you are aware of a crowd of people, they are those she has met upon her journey through the Tarot images. They are all joined in celebration of her victory yet they are all aware that this is but the end of one journey and the beginning of another.

It is too the end of your own personal journey and you look about for your door which forms within the laurel wreath, it opens and you pass through back into your own time and place and the beginning of another journey.

THE SUN
XIX
III
THE EMPRESS.
XVII
WHEEL of FORTUNE.
X
THE HANGED MAN.

A Theory

One of the eternal questions humans ask is what is life? Another is what are psychic phenomena? I would suggest they are both expressions of the same energy, just as light and heat are in the material world, but of different wavelengths. This energy lies beyond the wavelengths which compose the physical world and can only be accessed through the inwardly focussed consciousness.

The material world we live in is composed of atoms. Electrons are the smallest of the three particles that make up atoms. Electrons are found in shells or orbitals that surround the nucleus of an atom. Protons and neutrons are found in the nucleus. They contain still smaller particles, which are called quarks. Quarks are as small as or smaller than physicists can measure. At this border the visible becomes the invisible, the material the immaterial, but this is a boundary only as far as human material investigation is concerned.

Strange effects occur at the extremes of the particle world. For instance, entangled particles are identical entities that share common origins and properties, and remain in instantaneous touch with each other, no matter how wide the gap between them. They can be separated by continents yet react identically. Does this not sound rather like telepathy?

We observe the physical Universe by means of light. We are equipped with eyes which enable us to perceive light. By means of our other inventions we can observe other radiations emitted by the Sun and other bodies in the Cosmos, and by observing the microscopic composition of those radiations. There are boundaries to the material universe such as the speed of light, beyond which the laws change and often become contradictory. For a convenient term we will call this world which lies beyond the physical limits the Lumen.

It is only through our five perceptive senses of sight, sound, smell, touch, and taste that we can know something exists in the external physical world. Yet we have another ability through which we can observe beyond the physical and that is consciousness. When attention is turned inwards, consciousness can become aware of things within the mind which do not have their origin in the material world. We term this state imagination and wrongly call it unreal. It is also possible to observe the physical world through the vibrations of the Lumen. This occurs in deep meditation and out of body experiences. Whatever and however we observe it, it is always a function of consciousness. Knowledge may be acquired via the Lumen and be received by consciousness via memory such as in recall of dreams.

Consciousness is a state of active thought and awareness. In the physical world external stimuli are received by the brain and projected into the external world. Internal stimuli from the Lumen are received by consciousness, although in a more tenuous manner than those of material origin. Thought is a radiation of the Lumen and can operate independently of the physical mind and body. Relaxation is the key which unlocks the entry to the Lumen. When observing by means of the Lumen it is as if we can observe in all directions, a 360-degree viewpoint. In my experience in contact with Beings of the Lumen they are not perceived in human form but as a field of scintillating geometric shapes. Communication is by a transfer of thoughts.

Human beings are conscious beings who live in a physical body built of atoms and animated by the Life Force. Consciousness and the Life Force reside in physical bodies while they are alive, at death both depart and return into the Lumen from whence they came.

I suggest the Lumen is composed of something which is of a vibrational nature which lies beyond atoms and their Quarks. And is as real as the physical universe but different. The Life Force and Consciousness are functions of this Lumen vibration. In normal life the two are bound into the physical body, but occasionally may become temporarily separated. In this state one is fully conscious, one has no body or eyes, yet can see one's surroundings and one's own apparently unconscious body. This state is sometimes called being in the Body of Light, yet it is not necessary to 'see' a body, one is just a state of being which can observe one's surroundings.

Just as in the material world we are governed by the laws by which it works, just so in the Lumen world we are governed and function according to its laws. We do not see in that state in the same way as by physical light, it is more like we see in dreams, indeed many dreams are experiences in the Lumen world while others are just located in the brain.

This inner Lumen world has its own brilliant light which can sometimes flood the visiting consciousness. I suggest it has always been the objective of all so-called spiritual practice to gain the ability to experience this Lumen world beyond the physical. Many Traditions tell of deeper states still and teach techniques for reaching them.

I suggest that creation emanates from the Lumen and is an ongoing process. It is a case of 'need creates' that a need for a certain function in the living world causes it to evolve in a species. Or for a property to appear in the wavelengths of matter.

Psychic phenomena have their origins in the Lumen and are the result of the ability of consciousness to perceive its vibrations. The ability to perceive psychic phenomena is part of the nature of human beings, indeed of animals and possibly all living things. Like most abilities it varies in individuals and can be ignored or developed.

The material world and the Lumen world are not separate or mutually exclusive. The reason we have found them to be so is because we try to apply the laws of one to investigate the other.

Only when we learn the laws of each will we begin to understand each in its own reality and that they are but aspects of each other.

Elizabeth Anderton Fox
March 2021

I see that there has come to be in me a form which is not fashioned out of matter, and I have passed forth out of myself and entered an immortal body. I am not now the man I was I have been born again in mind.

Hermes Trismagistus

Autumn Leaves

The freshness of Spring, with all its excitement of new beginnings, is long past. The fullness of Summer with its richness and warmth is a memory. The autumn leaves are falling.

There is a special beauty to Autumn, its colours are dramatic and fleeting, the trees blaze in a final glory before folding themselves into their winter sleep.

Now too everything bears fruit, all things ripen and come to their fulfilment and the seeds of the new spring are set.

Our own lives are lived against this background of change in the natural world about us, we move through the seasons taking part in the changes and the various festivals which mark the divisions of the year. So natural does this seem to us that we barely notice how many times we have moved through the cycles of the year and that our own lives too have moved through spring and summer. Suddenly we realise that we too are moving into autumn with its wistful feelings of gentle sadness and endings.

Yet if we pause and look, there are leaves of many glorious colours surrounding us.

There are the leaves of bright gold, the loves and friendships of the years which have matured with us and are now rich in understanding and companionship.

There are the warm coloured leaves of family and our domestic lives, the seeds too of young folk maturing and the promise of new lives to come.

There are the deep red leaves of accomplishments

in our chosen fields of endeavour which mark our contributions to the achievements of our world.

There are the withered leaves of disappointments and sorrows which fall to the Earth and yet become the rich soil in which the future will grow.

There are so many leaves which are the memories of our past summers and the contentment's of our present season.

Our autumn leaves remind us that ahead is the dark of winter, yet there are still other leaves upon the trees which remind us that some things endure the darkest, coldest winter and are still there, living and growing when the spring comes again.

There are the leaves which never fade but live and grow and accompany us through all the changes and seasons - these are the leaves of experience, of our spirits journey, our garnered wisdom - these are the leaves which never leave us, which are our immortality.

Elizabeth Anderton Fox

The Sacred Mountain

Humanity has ever looked toward the heavens above as the realm and home of the Gods. In the glory of the Sun's light by day and the depths of the star- spangled sky by night, our ancestors sought to find, and bring the strength and support of higher powers they called Gods, into their lives. To climb the highest mountain brought a feeling of approaching closer to these powers and so the mountain became the dwelling place of the Gods and the most sacred place in their known world. Sacred mountains have always been regarded as manifestations of the archetypal cosmic mountain which is thought to exist at the centre of the world, they have been seen since ancient times as access-points to the upperworld of the gods.

In Japan Mount Fuji is worshipped as a god in its own right, perfect in its proportions, breath taking in its beauty. It is, for Shintoists, the incarnation of the spirit of nature. Buddhists venerate Fuji as the gateway to another world.

There are five mountains sacred to Taoists in China. The Tao way is the balance between humanity and nature, and this can be experienced in mountains which are thought to diffuse "*vital breath*". They are the medium through which people communicate with the divine as well as with primaeval powers of earth. The mountain seems to breathe the divine breath. It is related to as a living organism, and this sense of a sacred force is also reflected in the four Buddhist sacred mountains in China - representing the four quarters of the universe. Feng-shui, (or the science of wind and water) traces the dragon current of this sacred force as lines across the landscape, in the form of yin and yang (female and male). Mountains embody the masculine (yang) force. These are mountains of power, force, and majesty. Seas and rivers and low places represent the fluid, feminine, 'yin' force.

Ayers Rock, in Australia, sacred to Aborigines as Uluru, is the sacred site of the Dream time when the world was created, and the mountain is the unifying centre of the "*dreaming tracks*" of the ancestors. The dream time is still present at Uluru for the Aborigine people.

The sacred mountain of Abraham's call and Jacob's "*house of God*", Bethel Stone has now become the most sacred stone of all stones, the sacred rock in the Mosque of the Dome of the Rock. This same place is traditionally venerated as the site of the beginning of creation, the birth- place of Adam, as well as the place of Christ's crucifixion and resurrection. It unites and exprcsses our sense of mountain and rock as sacred sites of creation, the energy of the life force and the place of transaction between heaven and Earth.

The "Ancient House," as the Caaba is called, is a cuboid measuring about 38 feet in length, 35 feet in height, and 30 feet in width. The length of each side wall varies slightly and that of the end walls by over a foot. In the southeast corner of the wall at a convenient distance above the ground (about five feet) is embedded the sacred and mysterious black stone or aerolite of Abraham. When first given to that patriarch by the Angel Gabriel this stone was of such strong whiteness as to be visible from every part of the Earth, but later, it became black because of the sins of man. This black stone, oval in shape and about seven inches in diameter, was broken in the seventh century and is now held together by a silver mounting. According to tradition, 2,000 years before the creation of the world the Caaba was first constructed in heaven, where a model of it still remains. Adam erected the Caaba on Earth exactly below the spot in heaven occupied by the original, and selected the stones from the five sacred mountains, Sinai, al-Judī, Hirā, Olivet, and Lebanon. Ten thousand angels were appointed to guard the structure.

What is decomposition, the Persian argues, but the natural process by which the material elements are given back to the sun, the author of all forms of life? For this reason, a corpse with its feet to the East, is placed on a slab of jasper, which is then deposited on the top of a high column, in the Tower of Silence, in order that it may be secure from the attention of unclean beasts. For several days the remains are thus left undisturbed, during which time the heat of the sun, attracted by the polished surface of the marble slab, dries up the fluids. When this state has been reached, the birds of prey--which have been wheeling round the body--now settle to consume the dried flesh, a sign to the mourners who are watching, that the debt due to the sun has been satisfied, and that the birds have come to bear away the soul to the place of spiritual bliss which awaits it on the summit of the sacred mountains.

In the myths of the Navaho it is said; The flood was coming and the Earth was sinking. And all this happened because the Coyote had stolen the two children of the Water Buffalo, and only First Woman and the Coyote knew the truth. When First Man learned of the coming of the water he sent word to all the people, and he told them to come to the mountain called Sis na'jin. He told them to bring with them all of the seeds of the plants used for food. All living beings were to gather on the top of Sis na'jin. First Man travelled to the six sacred mountains, and, gathering earth from them, he put it in his medicine bag. First Man and First Woman formed six sacred mountains from the soil that First Man had gathered from the mountains in the Third World and kept in his medicine bag.

As before they placed Sis na'jin in the East, Tso dzil in the South, Dook oslid in the West, and Debe'ntsa in the North.

They placed a sacred mountain, which they called Chol'i'i, on the earth; and they made the mountain, Dzil na'odili, around which the people were to travel. There were four Holy Boys that First Man called to meet him. He told the White Bead Boy to cnter the mountain of the East, Sis na' jin. The Turquoise Boy he told to go into the mountain of the South, Tso dzil. The Abalone Shell Boy entered the mountain of the West, Dook oslid. And into the mountain of the North, Debe'ntsa, went the Jet Boy. Now the mountains to the East and South were dissatisfied. The East wanted the Turquoise Boy and the South wanted the White Bead Boy for their bodies. There was quite a lot of trouble; the mountains would tremble as though they would fall to pieces, and it was a good time before they were satisfied. The other mountains were happy in their bodies and there was no trouble between them. And after this was done and all was finished, the Earth and all that was on it was stretched in the four directions so that there would be room for all. The people were told that they were to use the six sacred mountains indicated as their chief mountains. The place of emergence from the lower worlds was where it is now. The people could always see their great mountains above the lower mesa lands. When everything was finished a smoke was prepared for the mountains and the chants were sung.

Rising to 2510 feet (765 meters) near the town of Westport in County Mayo, the quartzite peak of Croach Patrick was a pagan sacred place long before the arrival of Christianity. For the Celtic peoples of Ireland it was the dwelling place of the deity Crom Dubh and the principal site of the harvest festival of Lughnasa, traditionally held around August 1 (until the mid-nineteenth century only women were allowed on the summit during this pilgrimage and childless women would sleep on the summit during Lughnasa eve in the hope of encouraging fertility). According to popular Christian stories, St. Patrick visited the sacred mountain during the festival time in AD 441 and spent forty days and forty nights banishing dragons, snakes, and demonic forces from the site.

According to pagan British as well as Celtic lore, Avalon was the meeting-place of the Dead - the point where they passed on to another level of existence. Not only was Avalon a hill surrounded by water, but it was also linked with *Caer Sidi* - the Faeries' Glass Mountain or Spiral Castle, where the natural energies of the Earth met with the supernatural power of death. In very ancient times Caer Sidi was described as the abode of Cerridwen, the enchantress who possessed the Cauldron of Wisdom, a goddess with powers of prophecy and magic.

Just as the sacred mountains ceased to be physical places and became elevated into mountains in the heavens, so in time the heavenly mountains became internalised and came to represent those spiritual heights which humanity seeks to ascend in its spiritual quest.

For the Alchemists, Rosicrucians and Kabbalists the sacred mountain became the internal mountain whose summit represented the fulfilment of their search for the Philosophers Stone and the Elixir of Life. This inner mountain was represented in complex symbolism.

The drawing **Mons Philosophorum** or the Mountain of the Philosophers appears among the Symbols of the Rosicrucians of the sixteenth and seventeenth Century, first published in 1785 in Germany. The drawing is accompanied by a text which describes the symbology of the picture.

Note. The illustration on the next page is printed in reverse with reference to the text.

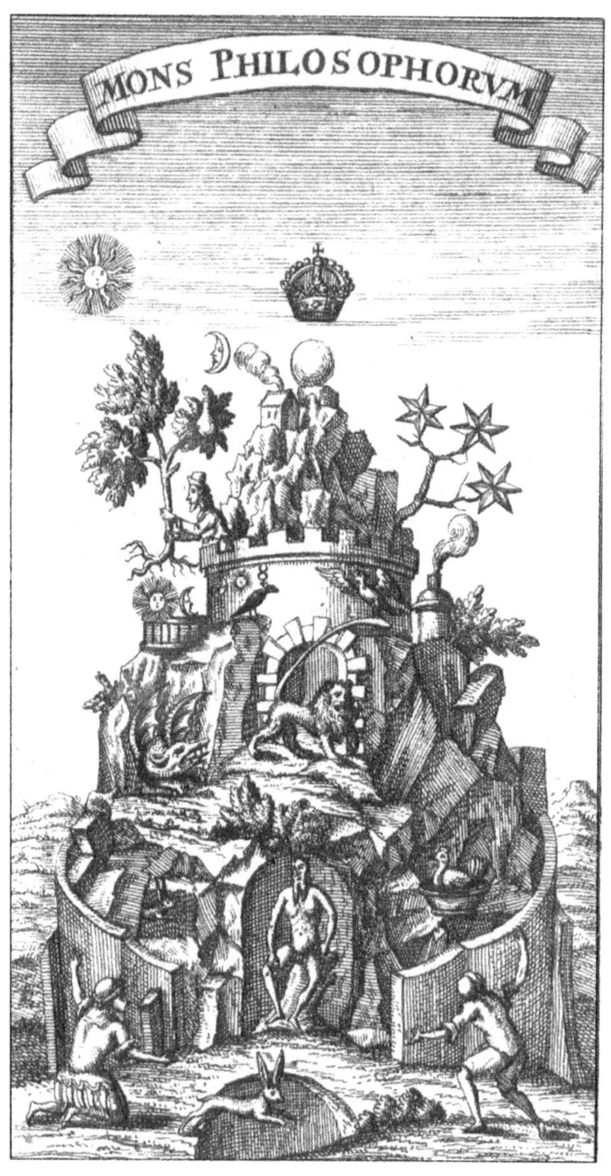
MONS PHILOSOPHORVM

The Soul of men everywhere was lost through a fall, and the health of the body suffered through a fall. Salvation came to the human soul through Iehova, Jesus Christ. The bodily health is brought back through a thing not good to look at. It is hidden in this painting, the highest treasure in the World, in which is the highest medicine and the greatest parts of the riches of nature, given to us by the Lord Iehova.

The Fall is the descent of the Soul into matter.

Jesus Christ can be understood either as the Saviour of the Christian religion or as the Cosmic Christ who is the great Power of Good which exists within the Cosmos. This Christos is the Son of God in that it is an agent of God, directing and aiding the development of Humanity.

The Christos can also be regarded as the Higher Self which resides within each person.

A thing not good to look at is that which is too great for humanity to gaze upon. It is the Cosmic Light. This Light is too intense for those in incarnation to look upon without harm to the physical vehicle.

The highest treasure is the understanding which frees the soul from dependence on physical manifestation and the limitations of Earth. It is Illumination. It is the attainment of the purpose of incarnation, the full development of the Soul.

The mountain referred to is the height of philosophy and mystical understanding. It is the spiritual climb out of the valley of materiality. The cave is a symbol for entering the deeper levels of the mind. It is the entry point into the depths of the sub-conscious.

Pator Metallorum is the Father of Metals, probably Mercury or Hermes Trismagistus. It can also mean the mine from which metals of great value are obtained.

The philosopher sitting at the entrance to the cave is also Saturn who represents the element of Lead, also darkness, the Inner Mind and the First Stage of the Hermetic Process.

But the Sophists in their Sophistic garb, tapping on the walls recognise him not.

The Sophists were paid teachers of rhetoric and philosophy in ancient Greece. It is a term applied to those who reason in a fallacious manner or quibble over arguments.

At the right is to be seen Lepus, representing the art of chemistry, marvellously white, the secrets of which with fire's heat are being explored.

The Lepus is a hare. This is a white hare. These were associated with magic and many superstitions. The hare was sacred to the Spring Goddess Eastre in Anglo Saxon traditions. It was associated with divination and omens. It is a symbol of speed and sometimes of healing. The hare is a symbol of mercurial volatility.

White is the colour of the second stage in the

alchemical process.

Fire was used in most Alchemical procedures to refine, purify and to extract the ultimate essence.

To the left one can see freely what the right Clavis Arlis is; one cannot be too subtle with it, like a hen hatching a chicken.

One can see that the Key of the Art to the method is patience. The hen and the hatching egg are an expression of the eternal transformation of the Ever Unchanging.

In the midst of the mountain, before the door, stands a courageous Lion in all its pride, whose noble blood the monster-dragon is going to shed; throwing him into a deep grave, out of it comes forth a black raven, then called lanua Arlis, out of that comes Aquila Alba.

The Lion is the symbol of Divine Life, he represents the Sun and the outflowing of life in all its forms. He is a symbol of Vigilance and of Divine Guardianship.

In the ancient Mysteries the Lion was said to open the Secret Book.

The Lion is also the conscious mind and the animal nature which guards the door to the sub-conscious mind and knowledge of the inner realities.

The monster-dragon represents the spirit of evil and the earthly elements.

A Green Lion and a Dragon also signify the prima

material of the lapis (stone).

A Red Lion signifies the third stage in the alchemical process,

Out of the Entrance of the Art comes a Black Raven. Ravens represent a link between the human and the animal kingdom. They represent the Thoughts of the Deity. They are often the messengers between divinity and humanity.

The 'Raven's Head' is also the dark sediment that is left on the bottom of the retort in the process of distillation, this was equated with the Element of Earth in Alchemy.

Out of the door also comes a White Eagle. The Eagle is symbolic of courage and the theurgic art, (operation of Divine or supernatural agency in human affairs).

Even the crystal refined in the furnace will quickly show you on inspection Servum Fugitivum, a wonder child to many artists.

You do not need a crystal ball to see the fleeing servant.

The one affecting all this is Principium Laboris.

That which influences all this is the Great Work.

On the right hand in the barrel are Sol and Luna, the intelligence of the firmament.

The Sun and Moon shine over all and are the governing powers of the scene.

The Senior plants in it Rad, Rubeam, and Albam. Now you proceed with constancy and Arbor Artis appears to you with its blossoms, it announces now Lapidem Philosophorum. Over all, The Crown of The Glory, ruling over all the treasures.

The trees, which are planted by the Elder, the Wise One, and which grow on the Mountain are radiant, red and white. (The colours of Alchemy.)

As the result of constancy one reaches the dwelling on the heights, the Tree of Knowledge of the Art blossoms and one achieves the Philosophers Stone. Then does one reach the Orb of Dominion and the Crown of Glory is over all. There are many routes that lead to the summit of the Mountain of the Philosophers, each one must find the way best suited to their own nature. He who climbs a little ahead must reach back and assist those who are a little behind. And those on the lower slopes look upwards and are encouraged and inspired by the progress made by those ahead.

Those who have passed this way before us record their experiences, triumphs and failures for our encouragement and assistance. They leave routes and maps for the guidance of those who come after.

In a Rosicrucian document by Thomas Vaughan of 1651 it is said - 'There is a Mountain situated in the midst of the earth or center of the world, which is both small and great. It is soft, also above measure hard and stony. It is far off and near at hand, but by the providence of God invisible. In it are hidden the most ample treasures, which the world is not able to value. This mountain—by envy of the devil, who always opposes the glory of God and the happiness of man—is compassed about with very cruel beasts and ravening birds— which make the way thither both difficult and dangerous. And therefore until now—because the time is not yet come— the way thither could not be sought after nor found out. But now at last the way is to be found by those that are worthy—but nonetheless by every man's self-labor and endeavours.

To this Mountain you shall go in a certain night—when it comes—most long and most dark, and see that you prepare yourselves by prayer. Insist upon the way that leads to the Mountain, but ask not of any man where the way lies. Only follow your Guide, who will offer himself to you and will meet you in the way. But you are not to know him. This Guide will bring you to the Mountain at midnight, when all things are silent and dark. It is necessary that you arm yourselves with a resolute, heroic courage, lest you fear those things that will happen, and so fall back. You need no sword nor any other bodily weapons; only call upon God sincerely and heartily.

When you have discovered the Mountain the first miracle that will appear is this: A most vehement and very great wind that will shake the Mountain and shatter the rocks to pieces. You will be encountered also by lions and dragons and other terrible beasts; but fear not any of these things. Be resolute and take heed that you turn not back, for your Guide —who brought you thither—will not suffer any evil to befall you. As for the treasure, it is not yet found, but it is very near.

After this wind will come an earthquake that will overthrow those things which the wind has left, and will make all flat. But be sure that you do not fall off. The earthquake being past, there will follow a fire that will consume the earthly rubbish and disclose the treasure. But as yet you cannot see it.

After these things and near the daybreak there will be a great calm, and you will see the Day-star arise, the dawn will appear, and you will perceive a great treasure. The most important thing in it and the most perfect is a certain exalted Tincture, with which the world—if it served God and were worthy of such gifts—might be touched and turned into most pure gold.

This Tincture, being used as your Guide shall teach you, will make you young when you are old, and you will perceive no disease in any part of your bodies. By means of this Tincture also you will find pearls of an excellence which cannot be imagined. But do not you arrogate anything to yourselves because of your present power, but be contented with what your Guide shall communicate to you. Praise God perpetually for this His gift, and have a special care that you do not use it for worldly pride, but employ it in such works as are contrary to the world. Use it rightly and enjoy it as if you had it not. Live a temperate life and beware of all sin. Otherwise your Guide will forsake you and you will be deprived of this happiness. For know of a truth: whosoever abuses this Tincture and does not live exemplary, purely and devoutly before men, will lose this benefit and scarcely any hope will be left of recovering it afterward.'

The Four Elements - Air, Fire, Water, Earth.

Within the magical / mystical Traditions of Western esoteric work all manifestation is said to be based on the effects of the four great Elements of Air, Fire, Water and Earth.

Western conceptions of the meaning and use of the Four Elements can be mainly attributed to Aristotle but the ideas can be traced back through Greek, Hebrew, Egyptian, Persian and Assyrian Traditions.

The ancient philosophers worked with the proposition that all things came from the four Elements, **Earth, Air, Fire and Water.**

In ancient texts the Elements were regarded as existing in each of the Four Worlds of Creation.

From their most subtle form in the Divine World of Emanation called Atziluth, through the World of Creation of Briah, the World of Formation called Yetzirah and into the World of Action called Assiah, they were said to descend from the Unmanifest into the Manifest physical world.

This process is described in the Sefer Yetzirah, an ancient work of Creation in the Hebrew Traditions as follows -

Chapter 1. Section 8.
The following are the ten categories of existence out of nothing.

1) The spirit of the living God praised and glorified be the name of Him who lives to all

eternity, the articulate word of creative power. The spirit and the word are what we call the Holy Spirit.

2) Air emanated from the spirit by which He formed and established twenty-two consonants, stamina. Three of them, however, are fundamental letters, or mothers, seven double and twelve simple consonants; hence the spirit is the first one.

3) Primitive water emanated from the air. He formed and established by it Bohu (water, stones, mud, and loam, made them like a bed, put them up like a wall and surrounded them as with a rampart, put coldness upon them and they became dust as it reads: "He says to the snow (coldness) be thou earth." (Job 37, 6.)

4) Fire or ether emanated from the water. He established it by the throne of glory, the Seraphim and 0phanim, the holy living creatures and the angels, and of these three He formed His habitation, as it reads: "Who made His angels spirits, His ministers a flaming fire." (Psalm 104, 4) He selected three consonants from the simple ones which are in the hidden secret of three mothers or first elements, air, water and ether or fire. He sealed them with spirit and fastened them to His Great Name and sealed with it six dimensions.

Cornelius Agrippa

In his *"Three Books of Occult Philosophy"* written in 1509-1510, Henry Cornelius Agrippa writes extensively of the Four Elements. They are the foundation of his writings on Western Occultism. He states that all elemental inferior bodies are compounded from the Four Elements by transmutations and union. At the destruction of such bodies they are resolved again into the Elements.

In their material manifestations the four elements are mixed and seldom pure.

In Agrippa's system each element has two qualities-

Fire	→	Hot and Dry
Earth	→	Dry and Cold
Water	→	Cold and Moist
Air	→	Moist and Hot

After this manner the elements, according to two contrary qualities, are contrary one to the other as; Fire to Water and Earth to Air.

There are also opposites in that some are heavy and some are light;

Earth and Water are heavy and according to the Stoics Passive.

Air and Fire are light and according to the Stoics Active.

Agrippa states that each of the Four Elements are threefold;

First Order - **Pure Elements.**

Unchanged, unmixed, incorruptible.
The basis of all natural things.

Second Order - **Elements which are compounded.**

They are changeable and impure but capable of being reduced.

Third Order - **Elements which are not true elements but compounds, various and interchangeable.**

Through the intermixing and transmutations of these elements proceeds all effects natural, celestial and supercelestial, through them is gained knowledge of future events and of good and evil.

The qualities of the Four Elements according to Agrippa are -

Fire

Active. Bright, yet occult and unknown. Fire, in itself is one, boundless and invisible but in that which it receives it is manifold.

Celestial Fire gives life to all things, it is the source of the light of the sun and celestial bodies. It makes all things alive and fruitful.

Infernal fire consumes all, making all things barren.

In early times it was believed that good spirits, which are angels of light, are augmented by light and fire. hence in all religions and ceremonies light and fire were used to keep away spirits of darkness and encourage the presence of divine spirits.

Earth

Passive. Earth is the basis and foundation of all things material. It contains the animal, vegetable and mineral worlds.

Water

Essential to all life. It is used in religious expiations and purifications and considered indispensable to spiritual regeneration

Air

A vital spirit, it passes through all things giving life and sustenance.

Agrippa gives the qualities of the Elements in the soul as -

Fire - Understanding.

Air - Reason.

Water - Imagination.

Earth - The senses

The senses are again sub-divided as –

Sight Fire- Active, fierce, quick, angry.

Hearing Air- Cheerfulness, amiability.

Smell/Taste Water- Fearfulness and sluggishness.

Feeling Earth- Slow and firm.

Alchemy

Alchemy sees the Elements as substances and stages of matter. They are symbols for stages of the Great Work.

The ancient Alchemists, like the philosophers, worked with the proposition that all things came from the four Elements, **Earth, Air, Fire and Water.**

The mediaeval Alchemists believed that all physical substance consisted of body and spirit which when submitted to fire were separated into its constituents of ashes > body and smoke > spirit. They thus thought that by Fire they could liberate Spirit.

The Four Elements were not regarded as made of a chemical composition in the sense that the elements of science are, but are rather as symbolic subdivisions of matter and its action.

The Four Elements symbolise the four stages of matter: **plasma** (a form. a mould, also an ionised gas), **solids, gases,** and **liquids** each with its particular way of embodying energy in form.

According to the theory of Paracelsus, God created a universe with the Four Elements, but this quaternity was founded upon the trinity of three principles, **mercury, salt** and **sulphur**. This trinity appears extensively in Alchemy.

Modern Philosophers say creation stands on the framework of carbon, hydrogen, oxygen and nitrogen. So the ancient elements have become metamorphosed into oxygen for Air, carbon for Earth, hydrogen for Water and nitrogen for Fire.

Tatwas

A very ancient system of India known as the Tatwas also uses the symbolism of the Four Elements. The constituents of the five-fold stream of the Tatwic current, which is said to underlie Creation, correspond to the Four Elements and Spirit, are in fact the ethereal or astral forms of the Elements.

Five Streams Symbol	Colour	Element
Akasha/Egg Shape	Deep Purple	Spirit
Vayu/Sphere	Blue	Air
Tejas/Triangle, Apex Up	Flame Red	Fire
Apas/Crescent	Silver	Water
Prithivi/Square	Gold	Earth

Hermetic

During the fourteenth to the sixteenth Centuries amid the Renaissance of learning in Europe, there appeared many writings which were attributed to Hermes Trismegistus and said to belong to the ancient wisdom of Egypt.

The Four Elements are used extensively in these writings which in turn are the foundation for much of the magical, occult, and esoteric theories and practice of the West.

The qualities of the Four Elements in the Hermetic system are -

Air - Free, hot, and moist

Fire - Active, hot, and dry.

Water - Fluid, cold and moist

Earth - Passive, solid, cold, and dry

Elementals

The Elementary Spirits or Elementals are said to be unseen intelligences who inhabit the four elements of the finest essences of which they are composed. The Spirits for each of the elements are as follows -

Sylphs

They control the air element and are believed to live among the clouds and on mountain tops. They are the highest of the Elementals, air being the highest in vibratory rate.

Their King is **PARALDA**. To the Sylphs was given the eastern corner of creation.

Said to be mirthful, changeable, and eccentric.

They are the invisible but ever present powers in the intellectual activity of the universe.

Salamanders

They control the fire element and are considered to be the strongest and most powerful of the Elementals. They have as their ruler a magnificent flaming spirit called **DJIN**, terrible and awe inspiring in appearance.

To the Salamanders was given the southern corner of creation.

In both man and nature, the Salamanders are said to work through the emotional aspect by means of the body heat, the liver, and the blood stream. Without their assistance there would be no warmth.

Fire requires Air in order to burn, so they are the two positive Elements. Water and Earth both extinguish Fire and so they are the two negative Elements.

Undines

They control and live in the water element. Portrayed as beautiful and graceful. There are many forms of water spirits such as naiads, nymphs, and sprites. Their ruler is **NECKSA.**

To the Undines was given the western corner of creation.

They are said to be vital and emotional and friendly to humans.

Gnomes

They control the material earth, its rocks, and minerals. They live in caves and forests. Other forms of gnomes are satyrs, pans, dryads, and elves. They are said to have the power of controlling their stature at will. Their ruler is **GOB**.

To the Gnomes was given the northern corner of creation. Said to hoard. They are not unfriendly to humans are said to be unpredictable.

Arthurian Myths

In the stories of King Arthur which are a rich part of the mythologies of the British Isles, the Knights of the Round Table are also representative of the elements, these are- Galahad equates with Air, Percival with Fire, Gawain with Water and Lancelot with Earth.

The Four Seasons

In nature each season is assigned to one of the four elements as follows;

Spring is Air, Summer, Fire, Autumn Water and Winter Earth.

Zodiacal Signs Assigned to the Elements

The twelve star signs into which the stars of the 360° of the band of the Zodiac are divided play a very important role in esoteric studies. The ways in which these are assigned to the Four Elements are-

The Four Cardinal Signs of the Zodiac

The Power. Serpents, The Initiators

Aries	Fire	Equinox
Cancer	Water	Solstice
Libra	Air	Equinox
Capricorn	Earth	Solstice

The Four Fixed Signs of the Zodiac

The Perfectors

Taurus	Earth	Beltane
Leo	Fire	Lammas
Scorpio	Water	Samhain
Aquarius	Air	Imbolc

The Four Mutable Signs of the Zodiac

The Developers.

Gemini	Air
Virgo	Earth
Sagittarius	Fire
Pisces	Water

Air

Gemini, Libra, Aquarius

PRINCIPLES of Mobility and Intermixing.

Gemini, the sign of the blossoming of new life.

Libra, the sign of balanced harmony.

Aquarius, the sign of new awakenings.

Fire

Aries, Leo, Sagittarius

PRINCIPLES of Light or Energy

Aries, the sign of birth and beginnings,

Leo the sign of maturity

Sagittarius the sign of old age and dying.

Water

Cancer, Scorpio, Pisces

PRINCIPLES OF Fluidity and Melting

Cancer, the sign of consolidation and advancement

Scorpio, the sign of preparation and transformation.

Pisces, the sign of synthesis and resolution.

Earth

Taurus, Virgo, Capricorn

PRINCIPLES of Solidification and organisation

Taurus, the sign of the creation of new life

and regeneration.

Virgo, the sign of full growth and harvesting.

Capricorn, the sign of rest and purpose achieved.

Seasonal festivals

As is seen above, the familiar four divisions of the year into the winter and summer solstice (when the sun is at its most southerly and northerly position respectively in the northern hemisphere) and the spring and autumn equinox (when the day and night are of equal length) mark the points at which the Sun is in a particular CARDINAL sign of the zodiac during the year.

These significant times have always been important in religious and secular life and it was the role of the early priesthoods to keep records and inform of their occurrence.

Less familiar, but still kept as festivals in some traditions, are the Celtic Fire Festivals. They fall on the cross quarters of the year at the mid-points between the equinoxes and the solstices These are in the **Fixed Signs (The Perfectors)**

Aquarius	Air	2nd February	Imbolc
Taurus	Earth	30th April	Beltane
Leo	Fire	1st/2nd August	Lammas Lugnasadh
Scorpio	Water	31st October	Samhain

February - IMBOLC, when the solar light is re-born and gaining in strength.

May – BELTANE, when the solar light is approaching full strength and all life is renewed.

August – LAMMAS, when the solar light is just past full strength and all nature is at the peak of fruition and maturity

November - SAMHAIN, when the solar light is dying and the light within is reborn.

Signs of the Fire Festivals and correspondences-

February - Aquarius, the Man, The Water Bearer and Matthew.

May Eve - Taurus, The Bull and Luke.

August - Leo, The Lion and Mark.

October - Scorpio, The Eagle and John.

Because of the procession of the spring equinox through the signs of the zodiac, which in our time is leaving the sign of Pisces and entering Aquarius, these Fire festivals now fall at the cross quarters. But in the calendar of the Taurian age about 2000 B.C. they were the signs of the solstices and equinoxes of that time.

Tarot

In the card system of the Tarot the twenty-two cards of the Major Arcana are assigned to the twelve signs of the zodiac and the seven ancient planets with the remaining three cards assigned to three of the elements. There is no card assigned to Earth.

Major Arcana - Fire/Judgement, Air/The Fool, Water/Hanged Man.

Minor Arcana - Swords/Air, Wands/Fire, Cups/Water, Discs/Earth.

In some packs the attributions are changed to Swords/Fire, Wands/Air.

Temple Work

According to classical tradition, the Four Elements together make up the astral formulae according to which all things are tuned to the Universe. If the magician controls these powers then he possesses the key to creation.

In the Western Mystery Tradition as perpetuated by schools such as the Golden Dawn, and in the present day by the Schools which have developed from it, the Four Elements play an important role in all ritual and meditational work.

The symbolic correspondences used are as follows-

Element	Position	Colour	Archangel	Creature
Air	East	Yellow	Raphael	Man
Fire	South	Red	Michael	Lion
Water	West	Blue Green	Gabriel	Eagle
Earth	North	Brown Green	Auriel	Bull

The symbolical Magical weapons as used in rituals in each of the four quarters are-

Air - The Sword in the East

Fire- The Staff in the South

Water - The Goblet or Chalice in the West

Earth - The Pentacle and also the inscribed Pentagram in the North

Summary

The ways in which the Four Elements are used in esoteric work are legion and you may discover many which have not been mentioned.

Below is a short summary of some further meanings and attributions.

Air

The Breath of Life in Man. The vitality of all life on Earth. The bearer of the Word and the cleansing winds of heaven.

Represents the principle of mobility and interrelation, intermixing, loosening up

That which permits the circulation of all substances. Circulates vitality and focuses energy.

Qualities - Intellect and intuition, gathering of knowledge

Action - Geometric, enlightenment, knowledge, sacrifice. Produces structure and order.

Represents - Knowledge, Structure, Order, and submission to Rule.

Functions - Activity, Light, clarity, Abstraction. Impulse and Repulse, The mental Nature.

Carries a spiritual force recognises by mystics as " The Breath of God." Creative and yet dispersive in nature.

In many of the world's religions and myths there is an association between Breath, Soul, and the Source of Life.

Air and birds, especially the Dove, have been associated with conception and the breath and air or soul.

In Christian belief the Holy Ghost is said to have descended on Jesus in the shape of a Dove.

Fire

Fire is the most versatile, creative and active of the Elements.

It is the most ancient and universal of spiritual and religious symbols.

It is, in a very real sense, the creative force of the Universe and the Light of the Spirit.

The Cleanser and the Destroyer. The flame which is the symbol of the life force in Man. The fire of the Sun which is the source and sustainer of Life.

Represents the principle of energy or light, vivifying and amplifying energy

Symbolises energy which moves in a spiral, thus any centre of force controlled by fire can be seen as a whirling vortex or wheel.

Qualities - Drive and ambition. Energy and enthusiasm. Spiritual, philosophic, energetic, forceful, active idealistic, temperamental.

Action - Cleansing, purification, power, truth, transmutation

Functions - Growth, Life, Illumination, Consummation, Transformation, Desire nature.

Fire was worshipped as a symbol of God in many of the ancient religions, in all faiths and at all times the light generated by flame has been regarded as representative of the Sacred and the Divine.

In Zoroastrianism which flourished for many centuries after the life of its founder Zarathustra (c.

628 - 551 B.C.), also known as Zoroaster, fire was regarded as the symbol of the God Ormazd, God of creation, light and goodness.

Down the ages Fire has been associated with many Deities such as Ra, Vulcan, Apollo and Helios.

In ancient Rome the Sacred Fire was worshipped in the Temples of the Goddess Vesta. Her Priestesses, the Vestal Virgins, were among the most highly respected and honoured citizens of that mighty and powerful Republic and Empire.

Fire is visible and invisible, discernible and indiscernible - a physical flame and also a spiritual ethereal flame manifesting through that material substantial flame.

In all esoteric teachings many symbols have been used to represent Fire. The most important have always been the Sun, the Flame, and the Sacred Fire.

In Eastern traditions Fire is represented by a red triangle and it is called Agni. The painter, poet, writer, and philosopher Nicholas Reorich was particularly associated with Agni Yoga which considers Fire as the central force of life, spirit and the Universe.

Fire is the symbol of regeneration in man, of skill, will, initiative, drive, energy, strength, and forcefulness of character. Its action is transmutation and transformation.

But above all Fire is Spirit, it is the Life Force in Creation. It is the purifier and the sustainer. It is the Sun behind the Sun; it is the agent of the Most High and the Light of God.

Water

The fertilising rain, the oceans and seas, the rivers of the land and all fluids which are the fountains of life.

Represents fluidity, melting and soaking up of energy, sensitising, joining, and causing energy to flow together.

Represents the "seed" of all things, the pearl of Great price, the secret vitality of humanity.

Energy and emotion of self-awareness. Helps to attain wisdom and serenity, peace, and harmony

Qualities - emotional, deep, reflective, responsive, spiritual, and mystical

Action - Peace, adaptability, love, wisdom. Produces rejuvenation, understanding, tolerance and harmony.

Functions - Cleansing, Forms, Purifies, Fills, and empties, Depth and love, Emotional nature.

Represents Wisdom, Intuition, Peace, Understanding, Tolerance and Harmony.

Symbol for Life, Chaos and Destruction. The Fountain of Youth, the Spring of Living Water.

Earth

Symbolises. Solidity, foundation, and fruition.

Represents the principle of solidification and organisation, structuring and gelling energy. The symbolic virgin element, the natural matrix.

Gives positive and practical attitudes of work and purpose.

Qualities - practical, sensible, reliable, patience, stability

Action - manifestation, creation, solidity. Establishes a foundation and brings ideas to fruition.

Functions - Energies of solidity, Patterning, Steadfastness, Law, Shaping, Transforming through pressure, The physical nature.

Aether

The Fifth Element is not one of the traditional elements. It represents spirit, space, consciousness, and the emptiness within which all forms play. It is formless and all encompassing.

Its symbol is the Wheel and it is the top point of the pentagram of Man.

It is that which exists and evolves within the sphere of the Four Elements of the Mysteries.

Look for the bearers of Wisdom,
seek for those who are bringers of Light.
They speak from the depths of their knowing,
and prove what they say to be right.

Look in the eyes of the children.
In the dreams which they know to be true.
The memory they carry unclouded
will bring truth and knowledge to you.

Look for the ones who can travel
though the body in sleep lies a-bed.
For they tell us how life will continue,
when we to the world appear dead.

Look for the ones who are teachers
who can open the eyes of the mind,
which lead to the world of the spirit
that material men never find.

Look to the ones who can listen
to the small silent voice of the soul.
For theirs is the path you must follow,
if enlightenment is your goal.

About the Author

Born in Colwyn Bay, North Wales, U.K. Elizabeth Anderton spent her early years in Wales and later settled in Cheshire.

By profession an Ophthalmic Optician, she is now retired from active practice.

Having an interest in spiritual and psychic matters from an early age, Elizabeth joined the Ancient Mystical Order Rosae Crucis in 1962 and followed their system of home study until 1990. In 1979 she first made contact with local groups and soon became actively involved in the work of the Order serving as a Chapter and Grand Lodge Officer until her resignation in 1990.

From the beginning of the Order Militia Crucifera Evangelica in the United Kingdom in 1991, Elizabeth served as Marshal of the U.K. Priory until her appointment to the Sovereign Priory as Magister Templi of the Order in 1996. She retired from this Office in October 2009 having worked extensively with O.M.C.E. groups worldwide. From its beginning in 1991 Elizabeth served within The British Martinist Order both at home and abroad until her retirement in 2017.

In 1981 she was initiated into Co-Masonic Free Masonry, Le Droit Humane, an International Order of Free Masonry open to both men and women.

Since becoming a student in the 'Servants of the Light' School in 1982, Elizabeth worked extensively within the school and was a supervisor for the S.O.L. coursework from 1985 until her retirement in 2018.

During 1980 she met John A.B. Fox and from 1982 onwards they shared a working partnership of lectures and workshops which led to the eventual formation of their own 'Sirius' title in 1990, under which they presented workshops and seminars, both personally and organising them for many of the day's foremost Teachers. John and Elizabeth were married in 1992. After a short illness John died on 27th January 2002, this brought their long partnership in esoteric work to a close.

From 2002 until 2015 Elizabeth was co-presenter with Dolores Ashcroft-Nowicki, Director of Studies of S.O.L., in their series of thirteen annual Ritual with Purpose workshops.

Elizabeth now lives in Milford Haven, south-west Wales, and has retired from group work. *Rituals of the Light Within* and *Journeys in the Light Within* alongside this book, *Tarot Journeys* are now her contribution to The Work.

Titles from Megalithica Books

My First Book of Magic by Dolores Ashcroft-Nowicki

Books for young people are very important as they provide information about things like 'what we believe in'. Most traditions and religions have books explaining their gods, ceremonies, celebrations and special days. But there are very few for those regarded as pagans. But ours is one of the oldest if not the oldest belief system in the world. So I wrote this book for you, whoever is reading it. As a pagan you are part of a way of life that began millions of years ago. We have survived that long, and you, little witchlet, boy or girl , need to claim your inheritance. ISBN978-1-912241-10-1 Price: £10.99, $15.99.

Journeys in the Light Within by Elizabeth Anderton Fox

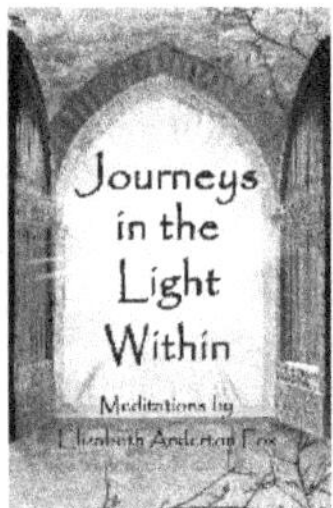

Journeys in the Light Within is a collection of writings, which were written mainly between 1982 and 2015, with some more recent writing. They were primarily designed for use within *Rituals of the Light Within* in workshop settings. They are now offered in the form of solo meditations; it is hoped that they will prove useful to others and interesting as reading material. The meditations are based on a wide range of spiritual and esoteric teachings. They contain elements of the Kabbalah as used in western mystery teachings. They are based upon some facts of astrology, science and astronomy. Above all, they are a reflection of a personal spiritual journey. ISBN: 978-192441-16-3Price: £9.99, $13.99

Rituals of the Light Within by Elizabeth Anderton Fox

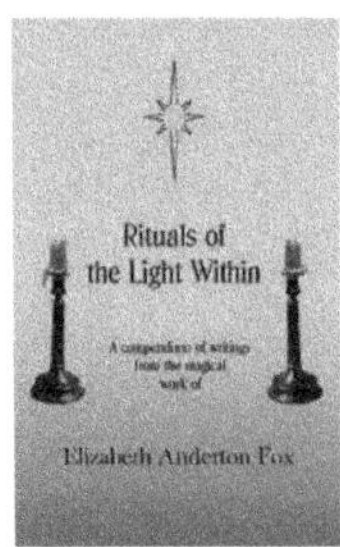

Rituals of the Light Within is a collection of writings by Elizabeth Anderton Fox, who has had wide experience in the Rosicrucian, Masonic and Western Mystery Traditions, and is a supervisor for the coursework of the 'Servants of the Light' school. The rituals in this book were written between 1982 and 2015, and were primarily designed for use by small and large groups in workshop settings. By publishing them in book form, the author hopes they will prove useful to others, as well as being interesting reading material for anyone drawn to the subject. ISBN: 978-0-9955117-3-6 Price: £13.99, $19.99

www.immanion-press.com

www.ingramcontent.com/pod-product-compliance
Lightning Source LLC
LaVergne TN
LVHW041155080426
835511LV00006B/604

9781912241224